COUNTRY
NEW ZEALAND
A Culinary Journey

Thanks to all the chefs and owners for providing the food and recipes that appear in this book – their help and encouragement was much appreciated.

First published in 2004 by New Holland Publishers (NZ) Ltd
Auckland • Sydney • London • Cape Town

218 Lake Road, Northcote, Auckland 0627, New Zealand
Unit 1, 66 Gibbes Street, Chatswood, NSW 2067, Australia
86–88 Edgware Road, London W2 2EA, United Kingdom
80 McKenzie Street, Cape Town 8001, South Africa

www.newhollandpublishers.co.nz

Copyright © 2004 in photography: Ian Baker with the exception of
Don Donovan: p22–23 (below), p120–121; Andrew Fear: p28–29
(below), p30–31 (above), p70, p80–81 (below)
Copyright © 2004 in text: Geraldine McManus
Copyright © 2004 New Holland Publishers (NZ) Ltd

Publishing manager: Matt Turner
Project editor: Fionna Campbell
Design: Dexter Fry
Food editor: Sarah Elworthy

Baker, Ian (Ian Gordon)
Country New Zealand : a culinary journey / Ian Baker ; text by
Geraldine McManus.
Includes index.
ISBN 978-1-86966-023-9
1. Cookery—New Zealand. 2. Food—Pictorial works.
3. New Zealand—Pictorial works. I. Title. II. McManus,
Geraldine.
641.50993—dc 22

10 9 8 7 6 5 4 3

Colour reproduction by PICA Colour Separation Singapore
Printed through Bookbuilders Hong Kong

ISBN 978-1-86966-023-9

COUNTRY
NEW ZEALAND
A Culinary Journey

NH
NEW
HOLLAND

NORTH ISLAND

Far North

• Mangonui

Rawene •   • Moerewa

• WHANGAREI

• Matakana

Auckland & Coromandel

Waimauku •   • Coromandel

AUCKLAND ●   • Hahei

Clevedon •   • Thames

• Te Aroha

Raglan •   • Matamata

HAMILTON

• Rotorua

Waikato &
Central North Island

• Taupo

Lake
Taupo   • Gisborne

New Plymouth   • Onaero
Oakura • Lepperton
Egmont village • Inglewood

Eastern North Island

Taranaki   • Napier

• Taihape

Feilding •

Palmerston North ●

Foxton Beach •   • Eketahuna

Manawatu &
Wairarapa

• Masterton

Marahau •   WELLINGTON ●   • Martinborough

Karamea •   Mapua •
Nelson • Picton •

Nelson, Marlborough
& Kaikoura

• Kekerengu

Barrytown •
Blackball •
Greymouth ●

West Coast

Canterbury

Lake Ianthe •

Taitapu •   ● CHRISTCHURCH

• Akaroa

SOUTH ISLAND

Lake Tekapo •
• Fairlie

• Wanaka
Cardrona •
● Queenstown

Otago & Southland

• Moeraki

Careys Bay •
● DUNEDIN

Invercargill ●   The
Catlins
Tokanui

STEWART
ISLAND

CONTENTS

INTRODUCTION

I have been photographing New Zealand in all its aspects for many years, but I never tire of its beauty and the way the rural landscapes change with the seasons. And it seems that food here in the heartland, in the way it is produced and cooked, just gets better and better. Therefore, following on from the success of *Simply New Zealand*, it seems to me there is room for another book that celebrates our beautiful scenery and good food – but this time with the focus on the countryside.

Many young chefs who trained in the cities have now dispersed and set up their own little places in remote corners. For the traveller this means that journeying around the land has become even more enjoyable, given that excellent dining experiences are now far more likely to be the norm. However, even if you are unable to travel, the pages of *Country New Zealand* still allow you to share in this country's riches.

Bon voyage – and bon appetit!

Ian Baker

FAR NORTH

Nowhere is far from the sea in the north. Coastal vistas of headlands dipping to golden sands and waves washing the shore are the backdrop to a tamed landscape of rural dairy and sheep farms. Sheltered harbours once provided a safe haven for sailing ships and early traders. And quaint seaside and country villages offer wonderful opportunities to enjoy the freedom of a relaxed outdoors non-city lifestyle.

Cape Reinga, at the tip of the North Island, fringed by both the Tasman Sea and Pacific Ocean, is renowned for its significance to Maori. The Bay of Islands was where, in 1840, the first signatures were gathered for the Treaty of Waitangi between Maori and the representatives of the British sovereign, Queen Victoria. The Treaty Grounds afford one of the most beautiful views over this expansive bay. As in the days of old, tall ships gather once a year in the Bay of Islands for a regatta. Polished topsides, timbered decks and square sails unfurl to catch the breeze. Throughout the year cruising boats carry tourists and racing yachts add streamlined action.

Unique to New Zealand, the native pohutukawa tree with its gnarled and twisted branches clings to cliff edges and graces beaches throughout the far north. It is New Zealand's Christmas tree, its flowers bloom in December to form a red halo above the green leaves, announcing the arrival of summer.

Food harvests are plentiful. Nearby fishing grounds teem with fish carried in by warm ocean currents from the Pacific. The north is renowned for its fresh seafood and shellfish, including mussels and oysters, and fish caught in both ocean and harbour. Citrus orchards and horticulture flourish in the north's sub-tropical climate. Kumara, the sweet potato which has been a staple of the Maori people for hundreds of years, is grown in Dargaville, the kumara capital. This potato variety is now a favourite in contemporary cuisine.

SLUNG ANCHOR RESTAURANT AND BAR, MANGONUI

Bluenose with Kumara Cakes, Grilled Asparagus, Red Onion Jam and Tomato Sauce

RED ONION JAM

2 red onions, peeled and finely sliced

20ml olive oil

100ml balsamic vinegar

1/2 cup brown sugar

salt and pepper

TOMATO SAUCE

1 brown onion, peeled and chopped

20ml olive oil

4 cloves garlic, crushed

1/2 cup mixed fresh herbs such as oregano,
   chives and parsley

1 can peeled, chopped Italian tomatoes

1 whole carrot

salt and pepper

KUMARA CAKES

3 kumara, peeled

knob of butter

1cm piece of ginger, grated

salt and white pepper

breadcrumbs for coating

vegetable oil for shallow frying

12 spears asparagus

olive oil

rock salt

800g bluenose, or another firm, white-fleshed
   fish, skinned and boned

butter for frying

beurre blanc with chopped fresh herbs for
   serving (optional)

To prepare the red onion jam, lightly sauté the onions in the oil. Add the vinegar and sugar and cook until the mixture forms a jam consistency. Adjust vinegar or oil to taste and season with salt and pepper. Spoon into a sterilised jar. This jam will keep in the refrigerator for up to 3 weeks, but warm through before serving.

To prepare the tomato sauce, sauté the onion in the oil until soft. Add the garlic, herbs, tomatoes and carrot and season to taste with salt and pepper. Cook until thickened, then remove the carrot. Place into a blender or food processor and pureé well. This sauce will keep in the refrigerator for up to 3 weeks.

To prepare the kumara cakes, boil the kumara in salted water until soft. Drain, then add the butter and ginger. Mash, then season to taste with salt and white pepper. Once the kumara is cool enough to handle, shape into 4 rounds, 80mm in diameter and 30mm high, coat in breadcrumbs and shallow fry until golden. Keep warm.

Preheat the oven to 200°C. Brush the asparagus spears with olive oil, then dust with rock salt to taste. Place in a roasting dish and grill or roast until just tender.

Panfry the fish in a little butter until just cooked.

To serve, arrange a kumara cake on each plate, pile 3 asparagus spears on top and arrange the fish on top of that. Place a generous spoonful of red onion jam on top of the fish and drizzle the tomato sauce and beurre blanc, if using, on the side.

SERVES 4

PREVIOUS PAGES Whananaki's rolling hills and small golden sand bays are great for walking, swimming or kayaking. This idyllic summer destination is on the coast about 26 kilometres off the main road north of Whangarei.

BELOW Rising to 460 metres above sea level, Maunganui Bluff provides spectacular views for walkers trekking along to Kaiwi Lakes. This nearby remote coastal hamlet overlooks the impressive west coast north of Dargaville.

TUNA CAFÉ, MOEREWA
Kumara Kao

2 large red kumara, coarsely grated

1 cup plain flour

2 eggs

about ½ cup milk (enough to give pancake
  batter consistency)

salt and black pepper

about 1 cup vegetable oil for frying

chutney or relish for serving

Mix the kumara, flour and eggs together in a bowl, adding enough milk to make a pancake batter consistency. Season to taste with salt and pepper.

Heat the oil in a large heavy-based frying pan. Place large spoonfuls of the mixture into the pan and press flat. Fry on both sides until golden brown.

Serve hot on their own with chutney or relish, or serve underneath crispy fried bacon, sliced tomatoes, softly poached eggs and hollandaise sauce (see recipe page 94) for Eggs Benedict with a difference.

MAKES 6 LARGE FRITTERS

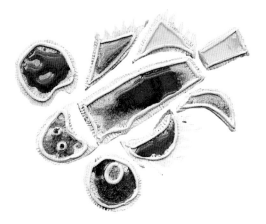

LEFT Maori handcrafts at the Tuna Café and Art Gallery in Moerewa, 6 kilometres west of Kawakawa, showcase both traditional and contemporary Maori art.

BELOW Early colonial buildings are scattered throughout the far north. Overlooking the Kerikeri Inlet, the historic Stone Store and New Zealand's oldest house, the Kerikeri Mission House built in 1822, are surrounded by gardens and lawns.

Fishalicious Pizza with a Freshly Cut Salad

Preheat the oven to 200°C, and grease a baking tray with the olive oil. Place the pizza base on the prepared tray. Spread the tomato paste and garlic evenly over, then the coriander. Sprinkle over a third of the mozzarella cheese and lay the spinach leaves flat before sprinkling another third of the cheese on top. Arrange large bite-sized pieces of lemonfish and the shrimps in a radial pattern and sprinkle the lemon rind on the fish. Finally sprinkle over the remainder of the cheese, ginger, dill and pepper to taste and bake the pizza for 10 minutes.

Place all the salad ingredients into a bowl and toss through the dressing just before serving. Serve the pizza hot with freshly tossed salad.

SERVES 8–10

NOTE: If using frozen shrimps, defrost them first to remove excess water.

LEFT Signal Point headland on the Hokianga Harbour once guided European sailing ships into a busy marine trading port. Now it's a quiet backwater popular for fishing. Huge sand dunes border the beach on the northern side of the harbour entrance.

1 tablespoon olive oil

35cm pizza base, uncooked

100g tomato paste

2 cloves garlic, finely chopped

large bunch fresh coriander, chopped

300g mozzarella cheese, grated

100g New Zealand spinach

300g fresh lemonfish, or another firm, white-
  fleshed fish

100g shrimps, fresh or frozen (see note)

rind of 1/4 salt-preserved lemon, sliced

2 tablespoons finely chopped fresh ginger

bunch fresh dill, roughly chopped

freshly ground black pepper

enough lollo rosso lettuce leaves to serve 8–10

mixture of red and yellow peppers (capsicum),
  finely sliced

radishes, cut into 8 pieces

large bunch of chives, chopped

large bunch of fresh flat-leafed parsley,
  chopped coarsely

spring onions, chopped coarsely

salad dressing (such as basil dressing) for serving

finely grated zest and juice of 1 lemon

finely grated zest and juice of 1 orange

185ml extra virgin olive oil

215g caster sugar

1/4 teaspoon salt

3 medium eggs

200g semolina

1 teaspoon baking powder

115g ground macadamia nuts

1 teaspoon orange flower water

4 tablespoons Cointreau

mascarpone, cream or yoghurt for serving

BOATSHED CAFÉ AND CRAFTS, RAWENE

Macadamia Citrus Cake

Preheat the oven to 160°C. Butter or non-stick spray a loose-based, 23cm diameter round cake tin and line the bottom with baking paper. Set aside a little of the lemon and orange zest for decoration, then put the remainder in a bowl with the orange and lemon juice, oil, sugar, salt and eggs. Whisk together with an electric beater or balloon whisk until light and fluffy and doubled in volume. Sieve the semolina and baking powder into a second bowl and add the ground macadamias. Add the orange flower water to the egg mixture and fold this into the dry ingredients, taking care not to over-mix. Spoon into the prepared cake tin and smooth the top. Bake towards the top of the oven for 40–45 minutes or until pale gold at the edges and a skewer inserted into the middle of the cake comes out clean. Remove from the oven and let the cake cool in the tin for about 10 minutes.

Drizzle the Cointreau over the top, then carefully remove the cake, still on its loose metal base, and leave it to cool on a wire cake rack for another 10 minutes. Remove the base and baking paper. Sprinkle over the remainder of lemon and orange zest. Serve wedges hot or cold with mascarpone, cream or yoghurt. The cake will keep in an airtight container for up to 4 days.

SERVES 6–8

BELOW Mists roll across the flat farmlands of Dargaville, a dairy farming area of small holdings. Northern dairy farms feed into the large cooperative dairy company that straddles New Zealand.

AUCKLAND & COROMANDEL

Sparkling waters lap the coastal reaches of the sheltered Hauraki Gulf waterway. Dotted by myriad islands, the gulf is a vast playground for recreational boating and fishing and adjoins the country's largest city, Auckland. Stretching from Mahurangi and Kawau Island in the north, to the inner Firth of Thames in the south, the gulf's eastern border is Great Barrier Island and the Coromandel Peninsula. Beyond is the vast Pacific Ocean.

Idyllic farmland overlooks seascapes of peninsulas of land jutting into the sea, forming a perfect picture of green countryside against a palette of blue sea and sky. Country lifestyle is dominated by 10-acre blocks where families enjoy the good life with their own horses, sheep and goats, yet are not too far from the city. Lifestyle combines with rural business on larger blocks for horticulture and serious farming. Both north and south of the city, fertile loams provide a vista of neat rows of vegetables and fruits such as onions, cabbages and strawberries. Late summer pick-your-own harvests draw city dwellers who flock to fill their buckets with fresh produce.

Also within a short distance of the Queen City's environs is a selection of notable vineyards with cellar doors open for tasting. To the west is the oldest wine area with many food trails and restaurants of note, while Matakana (north of Auckland) and Waiheke Island are both newer boutique wine regions. Sophisticated to country-style eateries provide a wide choice of options.

In the west the magnificent Waitakere Ranges are still quite rugged and relatively untouched. Native kauri trees were cut down in early European times for timber. Much of the kauri timber was used to build homes and these small timber cottages and villas still dot the landscape. Beyond the ranges are the wild wind-swept West Coast beaches of Bethells, Piha, Karekare and Muriwai.

HERON'S FLIGHT WINERY AND CAFÉ, MATAKANA
Flights of Fancy Feijoa Chutney

2kg feijoas, peeled and cut into chunks

600g sultanas

1kg pitted dates

1kg onions, peeled and finely diced

1kg brown sugar

50g ground ginger

50g curry powder

50g fresh red chillies, deseeded and finely chopped

20g salt

500ml water

Place the feijoas, sultanas, dates, onions, sugar, spices, chillies and salt into a large heavy-based preserving pan or stockpot. Mix together and add the water, then bring slowly to the boil. Simmer for $1^{1}/_{2}$–2 hours. Spoon into hot sterilised jars.

This dark, tangy chutney is perfect with a New Zealand cheddar, in a sandwich or with oatmeal biscuits, or spread under cheese melts.

MAKES ABOUT 12 SMALL JARS

PREVIOUS PAGES The Mahurangi Peninsula, north of Auckland, is near Matakana, known for vineyards and art and craft trails. Beyond is the water playground of the Hauraki Gulf.

RIGHT Mahurangi Harbour's secure and sheltered anchorage is frequented by weekend and leisure cruising boats. The picturesque navigable river runs right up to a marina in Warkworth township.

Rustic Fruit Tart with Tawari Honey Sabayon

TART

4 sheets filo pastry

melted butter

100g butter, extra

fresh fruit in season (apples, quince, figs, pears,
  peaches, nectarines, etc)

4 dessertspoons tawari honey

lemon juice to taste

TAWARI HONEY SABAYON

1 free range egg yolk

1 egg

1 capful dark rum

1 dessertspoon warm tawari honey

Preheat the oven to 180°C. Lightly brush the bottom of four mini tart tins or ramekins with melted butter. Cut the filo pastry into four squares just larger than the tins, using kitchen scissors. Brush each square with melted butter and stack on top of each other in the tins. Press the pastry gently into the bases of the tins and bake blind until just golden and crisp. Set aside to cool.

Just before serving, peel and slice the fresh fruit. Melt the butter in a saucepan and add the prepared fruit, honey and lemon juice and sauté gently until the fruit is tender.

To prepare the sabayon, whisk the egg yolk, whole egg, rum and honey at high speed in a bowl set over simmering water until thick and fluffy. A double boiler is perfect for this.

Assemble the tart by piling the warm fruit into the filo pastry shell and spooning over the sabayon. Serve immediately.

SERVES 4

NOTE: Tawari honey has a rich, buttery, almost chocolate-like flavour which is ideal for use in desserts.

BELOW Spring orchard blossom buzzes with bees providing sweet honey products then, later, the trees drip with apples and pears for the late summer harvests. Warm Auckland summers are perfect for fruit growing.

BELOW *Duder's Farm Park, Clevedon, is named after the family who have farmed this area since 1866. An hour's drive from downtown Auckland, the farm park is open to the public. Walking trails overlook the nearby Pohutukawa Coast.*

CLEVEDON CAFÉ, CLEVEDON

Peppered Cervena, Garlic and Gruyère Bread and Butter Pudding and Tamarillo Relish

To prepare the tamarillo relish, halve the tamarillos and scoop out the flesh into a large, heavy-based pan. Add the sugar, vinegar, garlic and star anise, then simmer gently for 30 minutes. Cool, then purée in a blender or food processor.

To prepare the bread and butter pudding, preheat the oven to 180°C. Butter or oil a casserole or baking dish and cut the crusts off the bread. Beat together the eggs, cream, garlic, cheeses, salt and pepper. Alternately layer the bread and pour over the egg mixture in the prepared dish until the bread and egg mixture is used up. Bake for about 30 minutes or until the custard is golden and set in the middle. Set aside.

To prepare the cervena, preheat the oven to 200°C and dust the meat with cracked black pepper. Heat the oil in a heavy-based frying pan and sear the meat all over. Transfer the meat to an ovenproof dish and place in the oven for about 7 minutes (medium–rare) or until cooked to your liking. Rest the meat for at least 5 minutes before slicing.

Serve the meat with the bread and butter pudding, tamarillo relish and reduced balsamic vinegar, garnished with fresh herbs.

TAMARILLO RELISH

1kg tamarillos

2 cups brown sugar

1/2 cup balsamic vinegar

2 tablespoons crushed garlic

4 star anise

BREAD AND BUTTER PUDDING

1 1/2 loaves sliced white bread

12 eggs

500ml cream

1 tablespoon crushed garlic

500g gruyère cheese, grated

1 cup grated cheddar cheese

1/2 teaspoon salt

1/2 teaspoon pepper

cervena Denver leg, about 800g

cracked black pepper

2 tablespoons oil

reduced balsamic vinegar for serving

fresh herbs for garnishing

Rice-filled Roast Peppers

6 large peppers (capsicum), 2 each of red, green
and yellow

¹/₂ cup vegetable or chicken stock

50g butter

¹/₂ cup short-grain rice

¹/₂ cup white wine or water

salt

2 tablespoons good-quality olive oil

1 small onion, peeled and finely chopped

2 spring onions, finely chopped

3 cloves garlic, finely chopped

1 tablespoon finely chopped parsley

1 tablespoon fresh thyme leaves

juice of ¹/₂ a lemon

1 tablespoon chopped pine nuts

3 anchovy fillets, finely chopped (optional,
see note)

salt and freshly ground black pepper

DRESSING

6 tablespoons extra virgin olive oil

3 tablespoons red wine vinegar

¹/₄ teaspoon wholegrain mustard

salt and freshly ground black pepper

Preheat the oven to 170°C. Roast the peppers whole for 17 minutes, then turn them over and roast for a further 17 minutes. Remove the peppers from the oven and place in a plastic bag to cool. Once the peppers are cool enough to handle, peel off the skins and cut off the tops, then cut open and flatten them, taking care to remove all the seeds. Set aside.

Heat the stock in a small saucepan until it is simmering. Meanwhile, melt the butter in a small deep casserole on the stovetop, add the rice and stir to coat well in the butter. Pour in the wine or water, then stir in the hot stock. Season to taste with salt (if you are using a commercial stock you may not need to add any salt). Remove from the heat and bake, covered, for 15 minutes at 180°C. Leave the casserole to stand, covered, for 10 minutes, then remove the lid, stir and cool.

In a deep medium-sized frying pan, heat 1 tablespoon of the olive oil and sauté the onion, spring onions and garlic slowly until the onion is soft and tender but not brown. Turn off the heat and add the cooled rice, parsley, thyme, remaining olive oil, lemon juice, pine nuts and anchovies, if using. Season to taste with salt and pepper and mix gently but thoroughly.

Lay a pepper out flat, inside up, and spread over a layer of rice mixture. Carefully roll the pepper up and cut it in half crossways. Arrange in a dish with the spiral side up. Repeat this with each pepper, alternating colours.

To prepare the dressing, whisk all the ingredients together in a small bowl and pour over the peppers before refrigerating.

This dish can be made a day ahead as the flavour will only improve.

SERVES 4

NOTE: Large Ortiz anchovies, available from specialty food shops, are recommended for those who are unsure about anchovies.

LEFT Early European settlement on the Coromandel left a legacy of colonial timber homes often located beside the beach. The sea provided access and was the major form of transport.

250g packet plain sweet biscuits

180g unsalted butter

500g cream cheese

$^1/_3$ cup icing sugar

1 litre fresh cream

1 $^1/_2$ tablespoons gelatine

$^2/_3$ cup boiling water

250g dark chocolate

finely grated zest of 2 oranges

THE ASSAY HOUSECAFÉ & WINEBAR, COROMANDEL

Chocolate Orange Cheesecake

Butter a loose-based, 28cm diameter springform cake tin and line the bottom with baking paper. Place the biscuits into a food processor and process until you have fine crumbs. Melt the butter in a saucepan and add the biscuit crumbs, mixing well. Press the mixture evenly and firmly into the base of the prepared tin. Leave in the refrigerator for 20–30 minutes to firm up or if you are in a hurry, place in the freezer for 10–15 minutes.

Using the whipping head of a cake mixer or a hand-held electric beater, cream the cream cheese and icing sugar together for about 10–15 minutes at a medium–high speed. Add the cream slowly to form a thick creamy mix. In a separate bowl melt the

RIGHT The bush-fringed Waiau River is one of many rivers plunging out of the Coromandel Pensinsula high country. Walking tracks provide access beside and over streams into the dense native forests that cover land too steep for farming.

gelatine in the boiling water and leave it to cool a little. Slowly add the gelatine to the cream cheese mixture until it is well incorporated. Divide the cream cheese mixture into separate bowls, one containing one-third and the other two-thirds. Melt the chocolate and add this to the larger mixture, then add the orange zest to the other bowl. Place both bowls in the refrigerator to firm up a little.

Once the chocolate and orange mixtures have firmed up, place spoonfuls of the chocolate mixture onto the biscuit base and alternate this with the orange mixture to create a marbled appearance. Return the cheesecake to the refrigerator until it is set, about an hour.

To serve, carefully remove the cheesecake from the tin to a large plate and use a hot knife to cut it into 8 portions.

SERVES 8

THE CHURCH RESTAURANT, HAHEI
Grilled Seafood Sausages

SEAFOOD SAUSAGES

100g snapper, tarakihi or another firm, white-fleshed fish

salt and freshly ground black pepper

150ml double cream

100g scallops, cut into small cubes

100g scampi or prawns, cut into small cubes

150g fresh salmon, cut into small cubes

100g tuna or hapuka, cut into small cubes

2 tablespoons finely chopped fresh dill

SAUCE

20g butter

¼ cup julienne carrots

¼ cup finely sliced leeks

¼ cup finely chopped celery

30ml dry white wine

100ml fish stock

100ml double cream

salt and freshly ground black pepper

grilled mussels and scallops to serve (optional)

To prepare the seafood sausages, place the snapper or tarakihi into a food processor and purée until smooth. Transfer the mixture to a large bowl, season to taste with salt and pepper and place the bowl over a basin of ice to keep the mixture cool. Gradually beat in the cream, then add the cubed seafood and dill and set aside to rest, covered, in the refrigerator for 30–40 minutes.

Using a piping bag or spoon, shape 8 sausages onto pieces of plastic food wrap to create sausage 'skins'. Gently poach the seafood sausages in a large pot of water for 5–6 minutes, then drain and cool them in cold water before removing the plastic food wrap. Place the sausages under a medium grill for 5–6 minutes, turning occasionally until they are golden brown.

To prepare the sauce, melt the butter in a heavy-based pan, add the carrots, leeks and celery and fry them gently until they have softened but are not brown. Add the wine and reduce by half, then add the fish stock and reduce by half again. Stir in the cream and simmer gently for 2 minutes. Season to taste with salt and pepper.

To serve, divide the sauce between four plates and arrange 2 seafood sausages and mussels and scallops, if using, on each plate. Serve immediately.

SERVES 4

ABOVE On the Pacific Ocean, Hahei's golden sand beach is named after the Maori chief, Hei. The beach is lined with bush, and at its southern end is a pa site enshrined in the Te Pare point historic reserve.

GRANGE ROAD CAFÉ, HAHEI

Roasted Salmon with Buckwheat Blini and Sorrel Cream

SORREL CREAM

¹/₂ cup sour cream

¹/₂ cup cream cheese

¹/₄ cup ricotta cheese

1 bunch sorrel, well washed

juice of 2 lemons

salt and pepper

BUCKWHEAT BLINI

1 cup buckwheat

1 cup flour

2 tablespoons yeast

1 clove garlic, finely chopped

pinch of salt, pepper and sugar

about 2 cups warm water

oil for frying

ROASTED SALMON

rock salt

oil for frying

4 salmon fillets, about 160g each

1 tablespoon butter

freshly steamed greens for serving

truffle oil for serving

reduced balsamic vinegar for serving

lime slices and chives for garnishing

To prepare the sorrel cream, place the sour cream, cream cheese, ricotta, sorrel and lemon juice into a food processor and blend until smooth. Season to taste with salt and pepper.

To prepare the buckwheat blini, place the buckwheat in a bowl and pour over boiling water to cover. Leave to soak until soft, about 5 minutes. Place the flour, yeast, garlic, salt, pepper and sugar in a separate mixing bowl and add enough warm water until the mixture is sloppy and a pourable consistency. Cover the bowl with plastic food wrap and set aside in a warm place until the mixture has risen, about an hour. Once the mixture has risen, gently fold in the buckwheat.

Oil four metal poached egg rings and heat a little more oil in a large heavy-based frying pan. Half fill each ring with batter and cook until small holes appear on the top, then flip and cook the other side. If you don't have metal rings simply pour the mixture into the hot pan to make 4 blini. Set aside.

To prepare the salmon, preheat the oven to 200°C. Heat a large, heavy-based oven-proof frying pan and add rock salt to taste, then the oil. Once the oil is hot, place the salmon fillets skin-side down to sear for about 45 seconds. Carefully turn each fillet over, place the blini in the pan beside the salmon and add the butter, then place in the oven to roast for about 5–7 minutes. The salmon should just be glassy inside when cooked.

To serve, warm the sorrel cream through and place a blini on each plate with steamed greens piled on top. Spoon over a generous amount of sorrel cream and place a salmon fillet on top. Finally drizzle over truffle oil and reduced balsamic vinegar to taste and garnish with slices of lime and chives.

SERVES 4

FAR RIGHT This quaint old building – just a few kilometres from Colville – was once a busy boarding house back in the days when goldmining was rife on the peninsula.

Sola Café, THAMES
Leek and Pesto Risotto Cakes with Tamarillo Chutney

To prepare the tamarillo chutney, place the tamarillos, garlic, vinegar, sugar, salt, cloves, peppercorns and allspice together in a large heavy-based saucepan and bring slowly to the boil. Simmer gently until the mixture becomes jam-like, stirring often to prevent sticking. Pour into sterilised jars and seal. This makes a substantial quantity of chutney which will keep well in the refrigerator.

To prepare the risotto cakes, heat the stock in a small saucepan until it is simmering. Meanwhile, heat the 2 tablespoons of oil and butter in a heavy-based saucepan, add the onion and garlic and gently fry until the onion is transparent. Add the rice and fry for 2–3 minutes. Add a ladle or two of boiling stock at a time, then stir, repeating the procedure as the simmering rice absorbs the liquid until the rice is cooked. It is best to cook the rice slightly more than al dente as this will help the risotto cakes to hold together when frying. Once cooked, set the risotto aside to cool.

Fry the leeks in the second measure of oil and add to the risotto, mixing well, along with the eggs and pesto. Shape into cakes and flatten before frying on both sides until golden brown.

Serve hot with tamarillo chutney.

SERVES 4–6

TAMARILLO CHUTNEY

2 1/4kg chopped tamarillos

1 tablespoon sliced garlic

300ml malt vinegar

450g sugar

1 tablespoon salt

1/2 tablespoon cloves

1/2 tablespoon peppercorns

1 tablespoon whole allspice

RISOTTO CAKES

2 litres vegetable stock

2 tablespoons olive oil

60g butter

1 onion, peeled and finely sliced

1 clove garlic, crushed

350g arborio rice

2 leeks, chopped

1 tablespoon olive oil

3 eggs, lightly whisked

3 tablespoons pesto

oil for frying

FAR LEFT A fishing trawler is tied up at the Thames wharf on the tidal estuary of the Firth of Thames. The Coromandel coast is renowned for its bountiful waters. Near the wharf, fish shops sell fresh and smoked seafood.

WAIKATO & CENTRAL NORTH ISLAND

From Waikato's lush verdant pastures to the steaming pools of Rotorua, this region has a diverse mix of outdoor country lifestyles. Fertile fields form New Zealand's best dairy farming lands and through the middle flows the mighty Waikato River.

Winding its way from the out-flow of Lake Taupo, this huge river plunges through the narrow rock chasm of Huka Falls and on to become a wide waterway flowing out to the west coast at Port Waikato. Once an important highway and byway for Maori, the river was used for travel by canoe as they traded, fished and foraged its surrounds. Now, on each bank, the land is grazed by hundreds of cows.

Artisan cheese-producers in this region include Matatoki's soft fresh cheese factory and several Dutch-style traditional cheese-makers based in Hamilton and Huntly. Katikati is a kiwifruit orchard belt where neat rows of vines drip over poles. Pickers walk beneath the vines collecting fruit in autumn.

Taihape, once known for its railway station pies, now has cafés with fresh cuisine tempting State Highway 1 travellers to stop enroute. While on the coast, appetites are driven by leisure pursuits in search of waves. Raglan's breaks are a world-renowned surfing mecca

Rich in cultural heritage and experiences, Central North Island is the heartland of Maori culture. In Rotorua there are places to try the unique and different indigenous foods and cooking methods. The hangi is a traditional cooking method using an underground steam oven with meats, seafood and vegetables cooked over hot rocks. Rewana bread is made plain or with added wild flavours of karengo (sea weed) and piripiri (fern fronds).

Polenta Loaf

1 medium-sized eggplant (aubergine)

olive oil for drizzling and frying

2 red peppers (capsicum)

4 green courgettes (zucchini)

6 cups vegetable stock or lightly salted water

300g polenta

100g parmesan cheese, grated

basil pesto

50g parmesan cheese, shaved

salad and red pepper (capsicum) sauce for
  serving

Preheat the oven to 180°C. Cut the eggplant into 1cm-thick slices, layer in a baking dish and drizzle with olive oil. Bake until the eggplant is lightly coloured, about 20 minutes, then set aside to cool. Roast the red peppers in a little olive oil at the same time the eggplant is cooking. Once the peppers are cooked leave until they are cool enough to handle, then peel off the skin.

Slice the courgettes into strips lengthways and fry in a little olive oil until they just start to brown. Drain on absorbent kitchen paper and set aside to cool.

Heat the stock in a large heavy-based saucepan until it is simmering, then pour in the polenta, stirring constantly to keep it smooth and lump free. The mixture will thicken and take on the consistency of porridge. Cook gently for 10–15 minutes, then stir in the grated parmesan and remove from the heat.

To assemble the loaf, oil a 9cm x 30cm loaf tin or terrine and spread a 1cm-layer of the polenta onto the base. Layer eggplant slices and a little pesto, then more polenta, then the courgettes, a little more pesto, polenta, red peppers, etc, until the dish is full, ending with a final layer of polenta. Sprinkle over the shaved parmesan. Bake for 40 minutes, then allow to cool.

Serve slices with a green salad and a red pepper sauce made by puréeing roasted red peppers and olive oil until smooth.

SERVES 4–6

PREVIOUS PAGES Rising above the high desert plateau are the active volcanic, snow-capped mountains of Ruapehu and Ngauruhoe. The Tongariro National Park is a popular recreational area which is an easy four- to five-hour drive from both Auckland and Wellington.

ABOVE Dairy country on the flat pastures close to Te Aroha, a country town nestled under the Kaimai ranges. Mists and clouds roll over the dense Kaimai-Mamaku Forest Park.

WORKMANS CAFÉ BAR, MATAMATA
Steak with Burnt Sauce

2–4 beef steaks: rump, fillet or any other cut
   of choice

2 tablespoons olive oil

4 cloves garlic, chopped

½ teaspoon cracked pepper

1 cup cream

pinch of salt

fresh vegetables or salad for serving

Panfry the steaks until cooked to your preference. Set aside to rest while you make the sauce.

Heat the oil in a frying pan. Add the garlic and pepper and stir until the garlic is lightly coloured and smells 'nutty'. Add the cream and reduce until the sauce thickens, then add the salt.

Serve the steak with the sauce and fresh vegetables or salad on the side.

SERVES 2–4

BELOW LEFT *Matamata's flat green pasture is renowned for its horse studs. Neat paddocks are edged by painted fences and, nearby, oval tracks are used to put thoroughbreds through their paces.*

TONGUE AND GROOVE CAFÉ, RAGLAN

Chicken Roti

To prepare the roti, place the flour, melted butter, warm water and salt into a large bowl. Mix together and knead well. Cut into 8 pieces and roll out into ovals on a floured surface. This makes enough for 8 roti.

To prepare the filling, heat a heavy-based frying pan over a high heat. Cook the roti for 5 minutes on each side, then brush the cooked side with butter. Once the roti are cooked, turn out onto a large wooden board.

Panfry the chicken and bacon together in a frying pan until cooked, then add the potato cubes to warm through. Place the chicken, bacon and potato on the roti and top with grated cheese and garlic aioli. Roll up and serve with homemade chutney on the side.

SERVES 1

ROTI

5 cups standard flour

100g butter, melted

1 ½ cups warm water

pinch of salt

extra ½ cup standard flour

FILLING FOR 1 ROTI

1 tablespoon melted butter

50g chicken breast or thigh fillet, cubed

2 rashers bacon

80g cooked potato, cubed

30g grated cheese

2 tablespoons garlic aioli

homemade chutney for serving

LEFT Plumes of native toetoe blow in the wind above surfing hangout, Raglan Beach, 48 kilometres west of Hamilton. The West Coast's steady break and curl attract local and overseas surfers shooting the waves.

MAORIFOOD.COM, ROTORUA
Nanny Cinny's Rewana Breads

3 cups lukewarm water

1 dessertspoon yeast

4 dessertspoons sugar

6 cups plain flour

100g piripiri (edible fern leaves), blanched or

    100g karengo (seaweed), (optional)

dipping sauces, infused oils or chutneys

    for serving

Butter or non-stick spray a large muffin tray. Place the water, yeast and sugar into a small bowl and whisk thoroughly to remove any lumps. Place 5 cups of the flour into a large bowl and gradually stir in the yeast mixture using a wooden spoon. (The key to this bread is starting with a sloppy consistency that is brought back to a soft consistency with the remaining cup of flour.) Mix through the piripiri or karengo, if using. Place the remaining cup of flour onto a clean bench and pour the sloppy dough on top. Gently knead the flour into the dough until smooth. Once the dough is smooth, cut it into 12 pieces, each about 115g and knead these individually in the palm of your

RIGHT Lake Rotorua has one major island, Mokoia, known for its romantic Maori love story of Hinemoa and Tutanekai. The island is now a refuge for endangered native birds and kiwi recovery.

hand by folding the sides into the bottom. Place the buns in the prepared muffin tray, ensuring all the tops are smooth. Place the muffin tray in the warming drawer or another warm place until the buns have doubled in size, about 35 minutes.

Meanwhile, preheat the oven to 180°C. Once the buns have risen, bake for 15 minutes or until golden brown. Remove from the oven and immediately flip the buns onto their sides in the tin so that the steam is released without making them soggy.

Serve warm or cold with dipping sauces, infused oils or chutneys. These breads are also delicious toasted the following day with poached eggs and hollandaise sauce (see recipe page 94).

MAKES 12 BUNS

REPLETE FOOD COMPANY, TAUPO
Kumara and Chilli Soup

Heat the oil in a large saucepan and gently sauté the onion, garlic flakes and spices until softened. Add the kumara and stir to coat, then cover the pan and cook over a low heat for 10 minutes. Add the chicken stock and water to the vegetables and bring to the boil, then simmer until the kumara is soft. Transfer the kumara mixture to a blender or food processor, add the cream and milk and purée until smooth.

Before serving, season to taste with salt and pepper and add the spring onion and parsley.

SERVES 6

1 tablespoon oil

1 medium onion, peeled and roughly chopped

1 teaspoon garlic flakes

¼ teaspoon ground cinnamon

¼ teaspoon ground nutmeg

½ teaspoon crushed chilli

1kg kumara, peeled and roughly chopped

1 tablespoon powdered chicken stock

3 cups water

1 cup cream

3 cups milk

salt and freshly ground black pepper

1 spring onion, chopped

2 tablespoons finely chopped parsley

FAR LEFT North of Lake Taupo a spectacular rock chasm squeezes the Waikato River, forming the magnificent Huka Falls. Every second more than 220,000 litres of water thunder over these falls.

RIVER VALLEY VENTURES LTD, TAIHAPE

River Valley Lodge Pizza

BASE

4 cups self-raising flour

1 cup cream

355ml lemonade

SAUCE

4–5 tomatoes, diced

1 clove garlic, crushed

½ onion, chopped

2 tablespoons chopped fresh mixed herbs

salt and pepper

TOPPINGS

use your imagination, but any or all of the
  following are delicious:

chopped ham

sliced mushrooms

finely sliced red peppers (capsicum)

chopped courgettes (zucchini)

chopped onion

chopped parsley

grated cheese

fresh green salad for serving

Preheat the oven to 200°C.

To prepare the base, mix together the flour, cream and lemonade to make a dough, then roll out on a floured board. Place on a well-greased oven tray.

To prepare the sauce, mix together the tomatoes, garlic, onion and herbs and season to taste with salt and pepper. Spread over the prepared base.

Sprinkle over your choice of toppings and bake for about 20 minutes until the cheese is melted and golden and the base is cooked through.

Serve with a fresh green salad.

SERVES 4–6

ABOVE *Wildflowers bloom in the rugged wilderness of the Kaimanawa Forest Park south-east of Lake Taupo. Wild horses run free in an area that attracts only a few hikers and hunters.*

FAR LEFT *South of the Central Plateau, the hill country farming near Taihape is rugged and demanding. When winter temperatures drop, snow can fall on nearby ranges and volcanic mountains.*

EASTERN NORTH ISLAND

Each morning the sun rises and shines first on the eastern Cape and Mt Hikurangi near Gisborne. The golden nurturing glow spreads across the fertile vines to ripen chardonnay grapes for this wine region's most recognised vintage. Food and wine are bountiful in the area near Gisborne and in the flat plains of Hawke's Bay, and each harvest is cause for celebration.

Large country estates with magnificent timber homesteads grace much of the countryside. Many of the outstanding sheep farms well-established in the rolling hill country have been passed down through five generations of the same family.

Rich in culture and heritage, the area's traditional Maori marae and meeting houses are some of the oldest in the country, many featuring significant carvings based on tribal history. The remote East Cape is called Tairawhiti, translating as "the coast on which the sun shines across the water". Inland, the forests and hills around Lake Waikaremoana, are the land of the Tuhoe people, often called the children of the mist.

An extraordinary earthquake in 1931 shook the town of Napier to pieces. It was rebuilt in just a few years in the art deco style. Beside the port of Napier some of the old warehouses have been turned into interesting cafés and restaurants.

Wonderful food and fabulous flavours abound in this region. Interestingly, Hawke's Bay is sometimes called the Bordeaux of the South Pacific because of the rich red claret-like cabernet sauvignon grapes that grow on the flat gravel plains, ripened by high sunshine hours.

Cafés and restaurants have a wide choice of freshly harvested local produce from which to create seasonal and regional menus. New vegetable varieties, fresh herbs and spices are also grown nearby, adding zany flavours to tickle the taste buds.

PREVIOUS PAGES Hill country close to coastal Mahia Peninsula in Northern Hawke's Bay. The Wairoa River flows and curves through the landscape to the coast.

RIGHT Tokomaru Bay's wharf is the longest pier in New Zealand and a well-recognised landmark on the East Cape. Once servicing an early shipping port, the wharf is a drawcard for visitors who are tempted to walk all the way to the end.

HIGHGATE, GISBORNE

Avocado Mousse

Blend or mash together all the ingredients by hand (do not use a blender) and chill for several hours.

Serve on lettuce leaves with fresh wholemeal bread or Melba toast, or seasonal vegetables such as blanched beans and cherry tomatoes for dipping.

SERVES 8

6 hard boiled eggs, chopped

2 avocados, peeled, stoned and roughly chopped

$^1/_4$ teaspoon chilli powder or chilli oil

1 onion, peeled and finely chopped

3 tablespoons chopped parsley

2 tablespoons freshly squeezed lemon or lime juice

$^1/_2$ teaspoon salt

lettuce, fresh wholemeal bread or Melba toast or vegetables for serving

1 cup cracked wheat

1 cup linseed

about 2–3 cups water

1.5 litres warm water

1 tablespoon granulated yeast

1 tablespoon Surebake yeast

1kg high grade flour

1kg wholemeal flour

1 $^1/_2$ teaspoons salt

$^1/_2$ cup soya bean oil

about 500g high grade flour, extra

melted butter for brushing

AVOCADO SALSA

1 ripe tomato

1 small red onion, peeled

$^1/_2$ cucumber

4 sprigs basil mint or basil, chopped

drizzle of avocado oil

freshly ground mixed peppercorns

1 ripe avocado

HIGHGATE, GISBORNE
Wholemeal Bread and Avocado Salsa

Place the wheat, linseed and just enough water to cover – there should be about three-quarters solids, one-quarter liquid – into a large saucepan. Cook at a very slow simmer over a low heat until all the water has been absorbed into the grains; this will take about $^1/_2$–1 hour. Keep it warm while you prepare the rest of the bread.

Mix the 1.5 litres warm water with the 2 yeasts and leave for about 10 minutes in a warm place until risen.

In a large bowl, mix together the first 2 measures of flour, the salt, oil, cooked wheat and linseed and the yeast mixture. Add extra flour until the correct consistency is achieved – the dough should be springy but not sticky. Turn out onto a floured surface (preferably wood) and knead for at least 5 minutes.

Divide the dough in half and put each half into a large well-buttered bread tin

RIGHT Remote East Cape is part of a touring route of 330 kilometres along the Pacific Highway from Opotiki in the north to Gisborne in the south. Near the Mahia Peninsula coastal lowland is sheep farming country.

(about 25cm x 15cm) or three smaller tins. Leave to rise in a warm place for about an hour until the dough has doubled in size.

Preheat the oven to 250°C. Once the dough has risen, brush the tops with melted butter and bake in the hot oven for 30 minutes until brown. Remove the loaves from the tins and return to the oven for a further 15 minutes. The loaves should sound hollow when tapped underneath. Leave to cool on a wire cake rack. This bread freezes well.

MAKES 2 LARGE OR 3 MEDIUM-SIZED LOAVES

Avocado Salsa

Finely dice the tomato, onion and cucumber. Add the basil mint or basil, avocado oil and season to taste with ground pepper. Halve and stone the avocado and spoon the salsa into the centre of each half. Serve immediately.

SERVES 1–2

HEP-SET MOOCH CAFÉ, NAPIER

Kumara, Spinach and Ricotta Filo Tart

Preheat the oven to 160°C. Grease a large rectangular tart tin with a little oil or non-stick baking spray. In a large bowl, beat the eggs with salt and pepper to taste. Add the ricotta, grated cheese, kumara, spinach, cream and pesto and mix together well.
Layer the filo pastry into the prepared tart tin, lightly brushing oil between the layers. Spoon in the ricotta mixture and sprinkle over the red onion and parmesan cheese. Bake for 30 minutes or until golden brown. Serve hot or cold with char-grilled vegetables and garnish with fresh herbs.

SERVES 4

6 eggs

salt and pepper

250g ricotta cheese

1 ½ cups grated mild cheese

2kg orange kumara, peeled, cut into chunks
   and cooked

2 cups cooked spinach, excess liquid
   squeezed out

1 cup cream

2 tablespoons basil pesto

6 sheets filo pastry

oil for brushing

1kg red onions, peeled and thinly sliced

2 tablespoons freshly grated parmesan cheese

char-grilled vegetables for serving

fresh herbs for garnishing

FAR LEFT Hawke's Bay is known for its grand pastoral stations which spread over the rolling hills. High sunshine hours and low rainfall regularly turn the green pasture to golden brown in summer.

Vegetarian Frittata

1 tablespoon butter

1 red pepper (capsicum), sliced

1 courgette (zucchini), sliced

1 clove garlic, crushed

1 dessertspoon sweet chilli sauce

4–5 large potatoes, peeled, boiled and sliced

2–3 large kumara, peeled, boiled and sliced

¼ medium pumpkin, peeled, boiled and sliced

½ head broccoli, lightly steamed

1 ½ cups feta cheese (see note)

16 eggs

3 cups cream

green salad for serving

Preheat the oven to 180°C. Butter a 28cm diameter springform cake tin and line the bottom with aluminium foil, then baking paper.

Melt the butter in a frying pan, add the pepper, courgette, garlic and chilli sauce and fry gently until softened. Set aside.

Layer two-thirds of the potato and kumara in the prepared tin, then spread over the pumpkin and broccoli. Crumble over the feta cheese, then layer the remainder of the potato and kumara on top. Finally spread over the pepper and courgette.

Lightly whisk the eggs and cream together and pour over the vegetables. Bake for 2–2 ½ hrs. Leave it in the tin to completely cool before turning out. Cut into wedges and serve with a green salad.

SERVES 10

NOTE: The feta can be substituted by ham, or diced cooked chicken and apricots.

WHITEBAY WORLD OF LAVENDER, NAPIER

Pumpkin, Spinach, Feta and Onion Muffins

Preheat the oven to 180°C. Butter or non-stick spray a large muffin tray.

Place the flour and baking powder in a large bowl and add the eggs, milk, onion, pumpkin, spinach and feta cheese and stir until just combined.

Spoon the mixture into the prepared muffin tray and sprinkle over the pumpkin seeds.

Bake for about 30 minutes or until golden brown.

Serve hot with a knob of butter and sweet fruit chutney.

MAKES 8–12 LARGE MUFFINS

4 cups flour

8 teaspoons baking powder

3 medium-sized eggs

2 cups milk

1 small onion, peeled and finely chopped

1 ½ cups cooked, chopped pumpkin

1–2 bunches spinach, blanched, chopped and
  excess liquid squeezed out

300g feta cheese, roughly crumbled

4–5 tablespoons pumpkin seeds

butter and fruit chutney for serving

BELOW Drifts of deep purple fragrant lavender at Whitebay World of Lavender, Eskdale, on the Napier-Taupo Highway. Lavender oil is made into soaps and bath oils.

TARANAKI

On the western coast of the North Island the solitary volcanic cone of Mt Taranaki/Egmont forms a sentinel on the landscape. Tipped with snow in winter, the near perfect cone shape is admired and revered, especially by visitors. Clad in dense bush, the mountain's slopes taper out into flat plains ideal for dairy farming where the cows graze on the greenest of grass. This region is recognised for its many dairy farms and the largest dairy factory in the country. Taranaki may also lay claim to being the cheese centre of New Zealand, where an extensive array of speciality cheeses are produced for both domestic and international consumption.

Surrounding the mountain is Egmont National Park, which is a year-round alpine playground for outdoor enthusiasts. In wintertime, it's the place for skiing and snow-boarding, then in summertime the bush and nature park is a favourite for tramping, mountaineering, rock climbing, rafting and abseiling.

Many farms were established by early European settlers, who cleared the land and built stately Victorian timber homesteads. Gracious living continues in these homes, often with extensive English-style gardens. Close to New Plymouth, the Pukeiti Rhododendron Trust's extensive grounds are recognised as the world's premier rainforest garden. The annual rhododendron festival held in spring draws people from around the world to admire the wonderful display of the rhododendron collection in bloom.

Off the beaten track favourite pastimes include 4WD touring across land and river and caving into the deep underground limestone caverns. Many west coast beaches are favourites for surfing and beach fishing. Fresh seafood and dairy food are favourite foods from Taranaki.

PASTA BASE

250g penne pasta

40g butter

2 tablespoons plain flour

1 cup milk

1 egg

salt and pepper

TOMATO SAUCE

1 tablespoon oil

1 medium onion, peeled and chopped

2 cloves garlic, crushed

425g can chopped tomatoes

¼ cup tomato paste

½ teaspoon sugar

350g marinated artichoke hearts

1 cup pitted kalamata olives

½ cup shredded basil leaves

1 small red onion, peeled and finely sliced

2 ½ cups grated mozzarella cheese

¼ cup freshly grated parmesan cheese

**basil leaves, black and green olives, red onion
 slices for garnishing**

fresh green salad for serving

WAIAU ESTATE CAFÉ AND WINERY, ONAERO

Mediterranean Pasta Pie

Cook the pasta in plenty of gently boiling, salted water until al dente, then drain and set aside.

Preheat the oven to 200°C and oil a deep 28cm pizza pan. Melt the butter in a saucepan and stir in the flour. Gradually pour in the milk, stirring all the time. Stir over a low heat until the white sauce thickens, then remove from the heat to cool slightly. Once the sauce has cooled a little, add the egg and season to taste with salt and pepper. Mix through the cooked pasta and press the pasta base into the bottom of the prepared pan.

To prepare the tomato sauce, heat the oil in a frying pan and add the onion and garlic and cook gently until the onions are softened. Add the tomatoes, tomato paste and sugar and simmer for about 10 minutes. Pour the tomato sauce over the pasta base and spread evenly.

Finally, top the sauce with the artichokes, olives, basil, red onion and cheeses. Bake for about 20 minutes or until browned. Garnish with the basil leaves, black and green olives and some extra red onion slices and serve hot or cold with a fresh green salad.

SERVES 8

PREVIOUS PAGES *Mt Taranaki's perfect cone rises to a peak of 2518 metres above sea level. The summit is a challenging climb of about five hours for fit trampers. Beautiful shorter walks wander through verdant forest to waterfalls and wetlands, many with excellent views.*

BELOW *Taranaki's west coast beaches are renowned for their surf breaks. The coastal road linking New Plymouth to Hawera in the south is known as Surf Highway 45.*

Chicken, Hummus and Sun-dried Tomato Panini

Mix the flour and seasoning together and dust the chicken breasts, shaking off any excess. Deep fry the chicken until it is crispy and the chicken is cooked right though. Slice each panini bread in half and spread the bottom half with the salsa and the top half with a generous layer of hummus. Sprinkle the grated cheese over the salsa and arrange the chicken and two pieces of sun-dried tomato on each chicken breast. Sprinkle over the spring onions and an extra drizzle of salsa. Lightly toast the paninis in a sandwich press or grill and serve hot with sour cream.

SERVES 2

LEFT Charming tiny timber country churches are found throughout New Zealand. Typically they are painted white on the outside and have a steep pitched roof. The interior is often beautiful, with varnished native timbers.

about 1–2 tablespoons flour

salt and pepper or a seasoning such as Italian herb or Cajun spice

2 chicken breasts

oil for frying

2 panini breads

about 2 tablespoons tomato salsa

2–3 tablespoons sun-dried tomato hummus

about 1/2 cup grated cheese

2 sun-dried tomatoes, halved

1 spring onion, finely chopped

sour cream for serving

SWEET PASTRY

250g plain flour

150g butter

2 eggs

100g sugar

3 tablespoons lemon curd

ALMOND FILLING

250g sugar

250g butter, softened

5 eggs

150g ground almonds

100g plain flour

2 teaspoons baking powder

50g whole almonds

LEMON SYRUP

1 cup sugar

2 cups water

finely grated zest and juice of 2 lemons

1 tablespoon honey

crème fraîche or whipped cream for serving

KAURI COTTAGE CAFÉ RESTAURANT, EGMONT VILLAGE

Sticky Lemon and Almond Tart

Preheat the oven to 165–170°C. Butter or non-stick spray a 22cm pie dish and line the bottom with baking paper. To prepare the pastry, rub the flour and butter together between your fingers until it becomes sandy in texture. Mix the eggs and sugar to a paste and combine with the flour and butter mixture to make a smooth dough. Roll out on a well-floured surface and line the prepared tin with the pastry. Spread the lemon curd evenly over the pastry and set aside.

To prepare the almond filling, cream the sugar and butter together in a bowl until pale

in colour, then gradually whisk in the eggs one at a time. Fold in the ground almonds, sieved flour and baking powder. Spread this mixture over the lemon curd in the prepared pastry case and decorate the top with the whole almonds. Bake for 40–45 minutes until golden on top.

While the tart is cooking, prepare the lemon syrup. Dissolve the sugar and water in a saucepan and bring to the boil. Add the zest and juice of the lemons, then boil until the syrup has reduced by half. Add the honey and set aside.

Once the tart is cooked, set it aside to cool before serving with warmed syrup and crème fraîche or whipped cream.

SERVES 6

BELOW The solitary volcanic cone of Mt Taranaki makes an iconic form above surrounding farmland. Vegetation varies up the mountain from towering podocarp rainforest to dense scrub, then tussock grass and alpine plant species nearer the summit.

BELOW Perfect rolled surf regularly curls on to Taranaki's coast carrying enthusiastic surfers along in its wake. Stretching down the coast from Raglan, the silver/black-sand beaches open to the wide horizon of sea and sky.

CAFÉ WUNDERBAR, OAKURA

Rabbit Just Wunderbar

Finely slice the onions and season to taste with salt and pepper. Heat a large frying pan and melt the clarified butter, then stir in the sugar. Cook for a few minutes until a light caramel forms, then add the onions and toss them around until they are well coated in the caramel. Pour in the balsamic vinegar and simmer over a low heat for about 20 minutes, stirring occasionally, until all the liquid is dissolved. Set aside to cool.

Preheat the oven to 190°C. Once the onions are cool enough to handle, stuff them into the prepared rabbit legs. Fold the ends over and close them with a toothpick. Season to taste with salt and pepper. Heat the butter in a large frying pan and seal the legs, browning them on each side. Transfer the rabbit to a roasting dish, place in the oven and roast for about 40 minutes. Once cooked, remove and rest the rabbit for 10 minutes in a warm place.

To prepare the crushed kumara, boil the kumara in salted water until just cooked. Drain. Stir in the butter and cream and season to taste with salt and pepper. Keep warm.

To prepare the glazed pears, cut out the core and slice the quarters in half. Melt the butter in a saucepan and add the pears. Cook over a low heat for 1 minute. Add the stock and reduce until thickened.

To serve, slice each rabbit leg in half lengthways and arrange both halves on top of some crushed kumara. Serve the glazed pears on the side and drizzle over the sauce.

SERVES 2

2 large onions, peeled

salt and pepper

2 tablespoons clarified butter

¼ cup brown sugar

½ cup balsamic vinegar

2 tunnel-boned rabbit legs (ask your butcher
  to bone them for you)

2 tablespoons butter

CRUSHED KUMARA

2 large orange kumara, peeled and diced

1 tablespoon butter

30ml cream

salt and pepper

GLAZED PEARS

1 pear, peeled and quartered

1 tablespoon butter

1 cup rabbit or chicken stock

GREEN CHEESE LICENSED CAFÉ AND CRAFTSHOP, TARIKI (INGLEWOOD)

Kumara and Apricot Filo Pie

600g golden kumara

1 tablespoon diced onion

1 teaspoon crushed garlic

1 cup milk

8 eggs

1/2 teaspoon dried oregano

1/2 teaspoon dried sweet basil

1 teaspoon salt

6 sheets filo pastry

oil or melted butter for brushing

24 apricot halves

about 3/4 cup grated parmesan cheese

Preheat the oven to 175°C and butter or non-stick spray six ramekins. Peel and dice the kumara and cook in boiling water until tender. Place the onion and garlic in a microwave-proof bowl, cover and microwave until soft. In a separate bowl, mix together the milk, eggs, oregano, basil and salt. Brush each sheet of filo pastry lightly with oil or melted butter and cut each sheet into 4. Layer each ramekin with 4 buttered sheets of filo pastry.

To assemble, fill the pastry-lined ramekins with kumara, sprinkle over some onion mix, sprinkle a little parmesan on top, then place 4 apricots on top of each one. Top up the ramekins with the milk and egg mixture and cook for about 40 minutes.

SERVES 6

BELOW At Pungarehu the Cape Egmont Lighthouse is a feature along the coast road west from New Plymouth. Originally a lighthouse in Wellington, it was transferred to Taranaki in 1881. Not open to the public, its light continues to guide offshore shipping.

MANAWATU & WAIRARAPA

Green and fertile rolling hills dotted with flocks of grazing sheep are the backdrop to this part of the country. Once the job of mustering these sheep was done on horseback; now, typically, farmers drive around their paddocks in a 4WD accompanied by their well-trained sheep dogs.

On the west coast black sand glints and glistens in the sunshine whilst the east coast's pale golden sand-hills are brilliant on the eye. The coast, and its river mouths and harbours provided seafood and water transport access for Maori who were the first to inhabit this landscape. Evidence of early Maori vegetable gardens is still visible on the coast close to Wellington.

Maori settlement was followed by waves of hard-working pioneers who duly tamed the land. The coast also played an access role for European settlers as people, timber for housing and farm buildings and even sheep were transported in and out by boat.

Lighthouses were essential beacons for this marine traffic and today some of them still play a role guiding shipping up and down the coast.

On offer is a smorgasbord of eating experiences – from country fresh spring lamb and venison to seafood from the coast.

200g seedless green grapes

330g butter

330g caster sugar

zest of 2 lemons

4 eggs

1 teaspoon almond essence

300g self-raising flour

³/₄ cup milk

140g ground almonds

icing sugar for dusting

fresh grapes and cream for serving

MARLOWS COFFEE HOUSE, FEILDING
Sunken Grape Cake

Preheat the oven to 170°C. Butter a 20cm diameter springform cake tin and line the bottom with baking paper. Wash and dry the grapes.

Cream together the butter, sugar and lemon zest. Add the eggs one at a time, beating well after each addition. Add the almond essence and gradually stir in the flour, alternating with the milk. Finally add the ground almonds. Pour the mixture into the prepared tin. Press the grapes gently into the top of the mixture so they are still visible and bake for 55–60 minutes, or until a skewer inserted into the middle of the cake comes out clean.

Dust the top of the cake with icing sugar and garnish with fresh grapes. This cake is lovely served warm with a dollop of cream.

SERVES 6–8

PREVIOUS PAGES Wooden red-painted woolsheds are typical farm buildings throughout the country. The Tararua Ranges provide high country for summer grazing.

BELOW The Manawatu region is a heartland of pastoral agriculture with rolling hills, deep gorges and fertile flat plains. Rural town centres serving the farming communities include Palmerston North and Feilding.

SUNDANCE CAFÉ, FOXTON BEACH

Gurnard and Scallops in Ginger Cream

Mix the flour, and salt and pepper to taste, together and lightly dust the gurnard and scallops, shaking off any excess. Heat the butter in a frying pan and panfry the fish and scallops over a medium heat until golden, then turn and cook the other side. Add the white wine and ginger, cover and simmer until just cooked through. Remove the fish and scallops, add the cream to the pan and reduce the liquid until it has thickened, then add a squeeze of lemon juice.

To serve, pour the sauce over the fish and scallops and garnish with the spring onions.

SERVES 4

flour for dusting

salt and pepper

4 fillets gurnard, or another firm, white-fleshed
 fish

12 scallops

100g butter

$1/2$ cup white wine

2 teaspoons freshly grated ginger

1 cup cream

squeeze of lemon juice

finely sliced spring onions to garnish

FAR LEFT The long stretch of Foxton Beach on the West Coast is popular for beach surf-casting. Fishermen drive their 4WDs along the beach to their favourite spot.

EKETAHUNA COUNTRY CAFÉ & CRAFTS, EKETAHUNA

Paua Fritters

3–4 medium paua

1 medium onion, peeled and finely chopped

2–3 eggs

1 tablespoon self-raising flour

salt and pepper

about 2–3 tablespoons milk or water

oil for frying

Blanch the paua by throwing the paua, shells still on, into boiling water for about 45 seconds – this helps to tenderise the meat. Remove from the pot and shuck the paua, then mince in a mincer or food processor. Stir in the onion, eggs and flour and season to taste with salt and pepper. Add enough milk or water to make a fairly thick mixture. Heat the oil in a frying pan, drop in large spoonfuls of batter and cook the fritters for 2–3 minutes on each side.

SERVES 4

Creamed Paua

3–4 medium paua

3–4 spring onions, chopped

about ³/₄ cup cream

¹/₂ cup grated cheese

3 tablespoons breadcrumbs

steamed rice for serving

salt and pepper

Preheat the oven to 125–150°C. Blanch the paua by throwing the paua, shells still on, into boiling water for about 45 seconds – this helps to tenderise the meat. Remove from the pot and shuck the paua, then slice thinly. Place the paua, spring onions and enough cream to cover the mixture in an ovenproof dish with a lid. Cover and bake for about 3 hours, then remove the lid and sprinkle over the grated cheese and bread-crumbs and grill for a few minutes.

Serve the creamed paua on a bed of rice. Season to taste.

SERVES 4

BELOW Wairarapa sheep farming country near Eketahuna is close to the coast where paua are plentiful.

Marinated Venison Back Steaks

3 tablespoons honey

4 tablespoons thick soy sauce

4 large cloves garlic, crushed

freshly ground black pepper

1 organic venison back steak, cut into
   thick steaks

oil for frying

2–3 kumara

¹/₂ teaspoon freshly crushed ginger

2–3 tablespoons butter

deep fried parsnip slivers for serving

fresh green salad and bread for serving

Melt the honey and place in a large flat dish with the soy sauce, garlic and freshly ground black pepper to taste. Add the venison steaks, making sure each steak is well coated in the marinade. Set aside to marinate for at least 4 hours – the longer the better, preferably overnight – covered, in the refrigerator.

Remove the venison from the marinade and drain off as much of the marinade as possible. Heat the oil in a frying pan over a medium heat and cook 2–3 steaks at a time. Cook for 2–3 minutes each side, keeping the heat moderate to ensure medium–rare to rare meat. Set the meat aside to rest.

Cook the kumara until just tender, then mash with the ginger and butter.

Serve the meat on a bed of kumara mash, garnished with finely sliced slivers of deep-fried parsnip and with a fresh green salad and your choice of breads.

SERVES 4

RIGHT Farmland stretches into the rolling hills at Tauwera near Masterton. Farm dams and lakes provide plentiful water all year for sheep and cattle and often are a habitat for wild ducks and waterbirds.

TOAD'S LANDING, MASTERTON
Individual Salmon or Ham Pies

4 large slices finely cut ham off the bone or

  8 slices smoked salmon

4 tablespoons cream

1 tablespoon butter

4 eggs

salt and pepper

chives for garnishing

toast and hollandaise sauce (see recipe page 94)

  or rocket for serving

Preheat the oven to 180°C. Butter or non-stick spray four muffin tins and line with the ham or salmon, allowing the pieces to hang over the edges of the tins. Heat the cream in a small saucepan with the butter, until the butter is melted. Divide the cream mixture between the lined muffin tins, then break one egg into each tin and season to taste with salt and pepper. Gently arrange the overhanging ham or salmon over the egg. Bake for 6–7 minutes until the eggs have set. Remove from the oven and rest for 3–4 minutes before turning out.

Serve the pies for breakfast or brunch, garnished with whole chives on toast rounds with hollandaise sauce, or on a bed of rocket as an entrée.

SERVES 4

BELOW In summer wildflowers bloom along country roads near Masterton in the Wairarapa. An annual spring scarecrow festival is a fun activity for farming families nearby, with scarecrows made from old pieces of material, straw and flowers.

Affogato Ice Cream

Place the first measure of sugar and the coffee in a saucepan and bring to the boil. Boil for 3 minutes to form a syrup. Meanwhile, half-whip the egg whites using an electric beater, then pour the hot coffee syrup in a steady thin stream over the egg whites while continuing to beat at high speed. Beat until the meringue mixture is very thick and has cooled.

Dissolve the second measure of sugar in the Drambuie. In a separate bowl, whip the cream to the same consistency as the meringue.

Finally, fold the sweetened Drambuie and ground coffee beans into the meringue mixture along with the cream. Pour into an ice cream container with a lid and freeze for at least 6 hours until set. This ice cream does not need stirring.

Serve in bowls topped with grated chocolate and biscotti or in an ice cream waffle cone dipped in chocolate.

SERVES 4–6

500g sugar

150ml strong espresso coffee

3 egg whites

100g sugar

100ml Drambuie

500ml cream

1 tablespoon finely ground coffee beans

grated chocolate and biscotti or chocolate-
dipped waffle cones for serving

BELOW Early European settlers cleared and settled the land for farming. Historic homesteads and delightful gardens are the result of their hard-working endeavours and prosperity.

THE OLD WINERY CAFÉ, MARTINBOROUGH
Chicken and Bacon Caesar Salad

Arrange the lettuce leaves in a bowl or plate and add the croutons, tomatoes, anchovies, chicken and bacon.

To prepare the dressing place the anchovies, garlic, egg, lemon juice, Worcestershire sauce and pepper to taste into a food processor. With the motor running, gradually add the olive oil in a steady stream until the dressing is thick and creamy. Stir in the parmesan and season to taste with salt.

Just before serving, stir the dressing and drizzle over the salad, then sprinkle over the extra parmesan.

SERVES 2–4 PEOPLE

2 cos lettuces, washed and dried thoroughly

1/2 cup croutons

2 tomatoes, sliced

6–8 anchovy fillets (optional)

2 chicken breasts, sautéed until golden brown
  and sliced thickly

8 rashers bacon, grilled until crispy and
  chopped

DRESSING

2 anchovy fillets

2 garlic cloves, crushed

1 egg, boiled for 1 minute only

juice of 1 lemon

1 teaspoon Worcestershire sauce

freshly cracked black pepper

about 1/2 cup olive oil

1 teaspoon freshly grated parmesan cheese

salt

1/4 cup freshly grated or shaved parmesan
  cheese for serving

ABOVE This white painted historic barn is still in use on pastoral station land in the Wairarapa. Early farm buildings and homesteads were predominantly built of timber.

THE OLD WINERY CAFÉ, MARTINBOROUGH

Venison Cutlet on Roasted Spanish Onions with Pinot Glaze

2 red onions, peeled

drizzle of olive oil

salt and pepper

1 tablespoon demerara sugar

20ml cabernet sauvignon, red wine vinegar
    or balsamic vinegar

1 tablespoon pine nuts, toasted

1 tablespoon currants

1 venison rack

1 cup pinot noir

1 tablespoon redcurrant jelly

50ml demi-glace or reduced beef stock

Preheat the oven to 200°C. Segment the onions, leaving the core intact and place in a single layer in a roasting dish with olive oil. Season to taste with salt and pepper and roast for about 15 minutes until the onions are starting to colour. Sprinkle the onions with the sugar and wine or vinegar, then continue to cook until the onions are soft and syrupy. Toss through the pine nuts and currants.

While the onions are cooking, sear the venison quickly in a heavy-based ovenproof pan then place it in the oven until it is cooked to your liking. Set aside to rest before carving. Place the wine in a frying pan and set alight over a high heat. Add the jelly and demi-glace or reduced beef stock, reduce the heat and cook until the sauce is reduced and thickened.

To serve, arrange the meat on the warm onions with the sauce drizzled over the meat and around the plate.

SERVES 4

FAR RIGHT Autumn's colours shade the vines outside Martinborough Vineyard's cellar door – open every day for tastings. Award-winning Pinot Noir is crafted in the small select Wairarapa wine region.

NELSON, MARLBOROUGH & KAIKOURA

Stunning scenery, first class wines and an abundance of freshly harvested and locally produced gourmet foods are standard fare at the top of the South Island. High sunshine hours and long golden summers provide the perfect climate and growing conditions for intensive orchards as well as vineyards. The expanses of Tasman Bay provide plentiful supplies of seafood including scallops, crabs and oysters. Local specialties from the Marlborough Sounds include greenshell mussels and salmon whilst off the spectacular Kaikoura coast pots full of crayfish provide a popular delicacy.

Nelson, named after the English admiral, is surrounded by fertile plains and rolling hills. The stunningly beautiful Marlborough Sounds was where explorer and navigator Captain James Cook took shelter while he was in this part of the world – many islands, promontories and inlets are named after him.

Coastal tracks follow the bush-clad shores but it is even better to view this labyrinth of hills, indented coast and deep inlets from a boat. Further south, Kaikoura, on the Pacific Ocean, is renowned for eco-tourism and sea adventures. Here it's possible to see dolphins, orca, humpback and giant sperm whales in the wild.

Lamb Rump on Blue Potatoes with a Roasted Garlic Jus

800g 'Maori blue' potatoes

800g lamb rump

salt and freshly ground black pepper

1 cup veal or lamb stock

20 garlic cloves, peeled

olive oil for frying

¼ teaspoon salt

½ cup red wine

1 tablespoon butter

olive oil and butter for frying

1 large yellow pepper (capsicum), sliced
  into chunks

1 courgette (zucchini), sliced on an angle

1 carrot, peeled and sliced on an angle

1 small head broccoli, sliced

Peel the potatoes if you like, or leave unpeeled, then cook in boiling, salted water until just cooked. Cool, then cut into large chunks. This can be done well in advance, even the day before.

Preheat the oven to 200°C. Season the lamb rump with salt and freshly ground black pepper, then seal all over in a very hot frying pan. Place the rump in the hot oven for about 5 minutes, then turn off the oven, leaving the meat in while you prepare the potatoes and vegetables. Turn the rump once or twice to ensure even cooking.

PREVIOUS PAGES Vines stretch across the stony river-flats of the Wairau River, excellent terroir for Marlborough's sauvignon blanc. The patchwork of vineyards, fields of garlic and cherry orchards is sheltered by a ring of hills.

RIGHT Bush-clad slopes dip down to the calm water of drowned valleys carved out by the ice-age in the deep Marlborough Sounds.

Place the veal or lamb stock in a saucepan and reduce to about half. Gently fry the whole garlic cloves in olive oil in another saucepan until brown. Add the salt, then deglaze the pan with the red wine. Reduce until almost all the liquid has evaporated, then add the reduced lamb or veal stock. Simmer and adjust the seasoning. Finish off the sauce by beating in the butter.

In a wok, heat the olive oil and butter together, then sauté the potato chunks, taking care not to overcolour them so they look burnt. Add salt to taste and set aside. Stirfry the remaining vegetables in the same wok until just tender.

To serve, place the potatoes and vegetables on plates, slice the rested lamb and arrange on the potatoes, then pour over the sauce. Aim to have everything ready at the same time so that the meat does not go cold or bleed on the plate.

SERVES 4

400g fresh salmon

HOLLANDAISE SAUCE

500g butter

4 egg yolks

30ml white vinegar

300g spinach

4 English muffins

8 eggs

MORRISON STREET CAFÉ, NELSON
House-smoked Salmon with Eggs Benedict

Smoke the salmon following the smoker's instructions (see note below). It won't take long – only 10–15 minutes or so as this is a hot-smoked method.

To prepare the hollandaise sauce, melt the butter in the microwave or on the stovetop, then place the egg yolks and vinegar in a food processor and blend together. Slowly pour in the hot butter taking care not to pour in the solids at the end.

To assemble the dish, wilt the spinach in a steamer for about 5 minutes. Toast the muffins and poach the eggs to your liking. Place a muffin on each plate, pile some spinach on top, then the poached eggs and salmon, and lastly pour over the hollandaise sauce. Serve immediately.

SERVES 4

NOTE: Basic smokers are available at sport and hardware shops. Use manuka shavings for this recipe.

FAR RIGHT ABOVE Hops, grown fresh for brewing, grow up strung-out lines in the Nelson region. High sunshine hours and fertile soils provide ideal conditions for horticulture near Nelson.

FAR RIGHT BELOW Honesty-box gate sales for freshly harvested orchard apples and pip fruit are typical along the country roads.

8 slices of prosciutto

4 corn-fed free range chicken breasts

1 cup white wine

SALSA VERDE

2 cups mixed herbs

2 cloves garlic, chopped

3 anchovy fillets, chopped

2 teaspoons capers

¼ cup lemon juice

¼ cup olive oil

4 tomatoes, quartered

8–12 gourmet potatoes (depending on size,
  allow 2–3 per person), cooked and sliced

16 olives

350g French beans (about 6 per person), topped,
  tailed, blanched and refreshed

MORRISON STREET CAFÉ, NELSON
Mediterranean Chicken Salad

Preheat the oven to 180°C. Wrap 2 slices of prosciutto around each chicken breast and place in a baking dish. Pour over the wine and bake for about 20 minutes or until cooked through.

To prepare the salsa verde, place the herbs, garlic, anchovies, capers and lemon juice in a food processor and blend until smooth. While the food processor is running, slowly pour in the oil in a steady stream until the mixture thickens.

To assemble the salad, layer the tomatoes, potatoes, olives and beans on four plates, slice the cooked chicken breasts in half and place on top of the vegetables. Pour a quarter of the salsa verde on top of each chicken breast. The salad is best served at room temperature.

SERVES 4

FAR RIGHT Nelson's farming valleys abut the many ranges of the huge Kahurangi National Park. The road from Nelson to the West Coast runs through the lowlands that lie alongside the park.

Lamb Rump with Tabbouleh Salad

LAMB RUMP

about 2 tablespoons olive oil

lamb rump, about 800g, trimmed of excess fat

salt and pepper

TABBOULEH

100g bulgar wheat

200ml warm water

1 cup chopped parsley

2 tomatoes, diced

1 small cucumber, diced

1/4 red onion, sliced finely

LEMON DRESSING

juice of 2 lemons

salt, pepper and sugar to taste

about 1/3 cup olive oil

Twice-baked Feta Soufflés and Pickled Eggplant
for serving (see recipes following)

To prepare the lamb rump, preheat the oven to 200°C. Heat the oil in a large, heavy-based frying pan and quickly sear the lamb all over. Transfer to a roasting dish and season to taste with salt and pepper, then roast in the oven for about 20–30 minutes, depending on how you like it. Remove from the oven and set aside to rest.

To prepare the tabbouleh, soak the bulgar wheat in the warm water for about 20 minutes until softened. Place the soaked bulgar wheat into a salad bowl and stir through the parsley, tomatoes, cucumber and red onion.

To prepare the lemon dressing, whisk all the ingredients together and set aside to infuse until you are ready to serve the salad. Just before serving, toss the lemon dressing through the tabbouleh salad.

Carve the lamb and serve hot or cold with the dressed tabbouleh salad, Twice-baked Feta Soufflés and Pickled Eggplant.

SERVES 4

BELOW Café windows open to the harbour at Mapua, 24 kilometres west along the Tasman Bay coast from Nelson. Waterside restaurants are popular places for dining out all day.

FLAX RESTAURANT AND BAR, MAPUA

Twice-baked Feta Soufflés

Preheat the oven to 180°C. Butter or non-stick spray six soufflé dishes or one large soufflé dish. Melt the butter in a saucepan and stir in the flour, then add the milk and whisk over a moderate heat until you have a smooth white sauce. Remove from the heat and stir in about 150g feta and the egg yolks. In a separate bowl whisk the egg whites to medium–firm peaks, then fold into the feta mixture. Spoon the mixture evenly into the prepared dishes and bake for 20 minutes.

Leave the soufflés to cool in their dishes, then turn them out into a baking dish, sprinkle with the remaining feta, pour over the cream and season to taste with freshly ground pepper. Bake until the top is golden.

SERVES 6

30g butter

40g flour

250ml cold milk

250g feta cheese, crumbled

3 eggs, separated

200ml cream

freshly ground black pepper

Pickled Eggplant

Peel and slice the garlic and grind to a paste in a pestle and mortar with some of the salt. Add a little vinegar, the chilli powder, turmeric and ground ginger and mix to a paste. Heat the oils gently in a large frying pan and fry the cumin and fenugreek seeds for about 1 minute. Add the garlic/spice paste and fry over a low heat until fragrant. Add the rest of the vinegar and salt, as well as the sugar, and mix thoroughly. Add the eggplants, chilli and fresh ginger and cook, covered, until tender. Cool slightly, then carefully spoon into sterilised jars. Ideally leave for 2 weeks before serving.

MAKES ABOUT 4 CUPS

1 clove garlic

1 heaped tablespoon salt

300ml vinegar

$\frac{1}{2}$ teaspoon chilli powder

1 teaspoon ground turmeric

1 teaspoon ground ginger

75ml grapeseed oil

25ml sesame oil

1 $\frac{1}{2}$ teaspoons cumin seeds

1 $\frac{1}{2}$ teaspoons fenugreek seeds

125g sugar

1kg Japanese eggplants (aubergine), split lengthwise from stem (or use regular eggplants cut into 2cm chunks)

1 sliced chilli

15g grated fresh ginger

ROASTED VEGETABLES

4 stalks celery

1 medium eggplant (aubergine)

1 head broccoli

1 pepper (capsicum)

1 red onion, peeled

3 courgettes (zucchini)

2 carrots

12 small vine-ripened tomatoes

handful of olives

1 tablespoon capers

about 2–3 tablespoons olive oil

salt and pepper

GREMOLATA

1 cup freshly grated parmesan cheese

1 cup finely chopped mixed herbs, such as dill,
  chives, flat-leafed parsley or whatever you
  have in your garden

finely grated zest of 2 lemons

sea salt and cracked black pepper

BALSAMIC REDUCTION

200ml balsamic vinegar

50g honey

PAN-SEARED FISH

1kg piece fresh groper or snapper, or another
  firm, white-fleshed fish, cut into 4 pieces

salt and pepper

1 tablespoon olive oil

fresh salad leaves for serving

HOOKED ON MARAHAU, MARAHAU

Pan-seared Fish with Gremolata and Balsamic Reduction on Roasted Vegetables

To prepare the roasted vegetables, preheat the oven to 180°C. Cut the celery, eggplant, broccoli, pepper, red onion and courgettes into bite-sized pieces. Cut the carrots on an angle into 2cm-thick slices. Salt the eggplant to remove bitterness if required, rinse and pat dry. Place all the ingredients onto an oven tray, season to taste with salt and pepper and drizzle with olive oil. Roast the vegetables for 7 minutes, then toss and roast for another 7 minutes.

To prepare the gremolata, mix together the parmesan, herbs and lemon zest and season to taste with salt and pepper. Set aside while you make the balsamic reduction and sear the fish.

To prepare the balsamic reduction, gently heat the vinegar and honey together in a saucepan until it is thick and reduced by about two-thirds.

To prepare the pan-seared fish, preheat the oven to 180°C. Season the fish fillets to taste with salt and pepper. Heat the oil in a frying pan and briefly sear the fillets until they are light brown on both sides. Place the fillets into an ovenproof dish and arrange the gremolata on top. Bake until just cooked, about 7 minutes for 2½ cm-thick fillets.

Serve the fish drizzled with the balsamic reduction on a bed of roasted vegetables and fresh salad leaves.

SERVES 4

*BELOW Golden sand at Kaiteriteri provides
a launching place for sea kayakers. Many
kayakers make a multi-day paddling
excursion along the coast of the Abel Tasman
National Park.*

HOOKED ON MARAHAU, MARAHAU
Scallop Salad with Basil Oil

To prepare the basil oil, place the basil and spinach into a blender or food processor and process until finely chopped. Add the garlic, parmesan, almonds and season to taste with salt and pepper. Drizzle in the oil in a steady stream while blending until the mixture is thickened and smooth.

To prepare the scallop salad, heat the oil in a frying pan until hot with a slight haze, then carefully place the scallops in the oil and sear both sides until golden brown. Add the capers, basil pesto and lemon juice and toss together gently.

Arrange the salad leaves on two plates, then arrange the onion, cucumber, tomatoes, peppers and carrots on top. Sprinkle over the herbs and place the hot scallops through the salad. Drizzle with basil oil and season to taste with sea salt and freshly ground black pepper.

SERVES 2

ABOVE Marahau's tidal reaches link the small settlement to the Abel Tasman National Park. Established in 1942, the park is named after the sixteenth century Dutch navigator, Abel Tasman, who named New Zealand.

BASIL OIL

1 cup fresh basil leaves

1 cup baby spinach leaves

1 teaspoon crushed garlic

1 tablespoon freshly grated parmesan cheese

1/4 cup sliced almonds

salt and pepper

about 1/2 cup olive oil

SCALLOP SALAD

1 tablespoon olive oil

12 fresh plump scallops

8 capers

1 teaspoon basil pesto

juice of 1/2 lemon

100–150g mixed salad leaves

1 small red onion, peeled and finely sliced

1/4 cucumber, chopped

6 cherry tomatoes, halved

1/2 cup finely sliced peppers (capsicum) and
  carrots

handful of fresh dill, torn

handful of fresh coriander, torn

vinaigrette or Basil Oil for serving (see recipe
  above)

sea salt and freshly ground black pepper

The Store, KEKERENGU
Lemon Citrus Muffins

MUFFINS

2 cups plain flour

1 cup sugar

2 heaped teaspoons baking powder

1 ½ teaspoons salt

finely grated zest of 2 lemons

100g butter, melted

1 cup lemon juice

2 eggs

TOPPING

50g butter, melted

lemon juice

½ cup caster sugar

To prepare the muffins, preheat the oven to 160°C. Butter or non-stick spray a 12-muffin tray. Mix together the flour, sugar, baking powder, salt and lemon zest in a bowl.

In a separate bowl, mix together the melted butter, lemon juice and eggs. Pour the wet ingredients onto the dry ingredients and stir until just combined. Spoon the mixture into the prepared muffin tray and bake for 30 minutes.

To prepare the topping, place the melted butter, lemon juice and sugar into three separate bowls. When the muffins are cooked, remove them from the tray and dip the top half of each muffin into the melted butter, then the lemon juice and finally the sugar.

MAKES 12 MUFFINS

ABOVE The sheltered Awatere Valley, 25 kilometres south of Blenheim, is known for pastoral farming, vineyards and outstanding gardens open to the public.

GRAVLAX

300g piece salmon

2 teaspoons rock salt

1 teaspoon cracked black pepper

1 tablespoon each: chopped dill, sugar
  and cognac

CRAYFISH

1 each: carrot, celery, leek, all roughly chopped

1 onion, peeled and halved

1 teaspoon each: cayenne pepper, peppercorns
  and salt

1 bay leaf

1 fresh raw crayfish, about 500g

PRAWNS

8 large fresh raw prawns

butter or oil for frying

$\frac{1}{2}$ cup whisky

MUSSELS

8 fresh green-lipped mussels

2 tablespoons each: garlic butter, softened,
  and breadcrumbs

CALAMARI

2 tablespoons olive oil

1 squid (calamari) tube, sliced into rings

3 cloves garlic, crushed

squeeze lemon juice

2 tablespoons chopped parsley

salt and pepper

FISH

1 cup basil

$\frac{1}{2}$ cup each: walnut pieces, almonds

2 cloves garlic, peeled

$\frac{1}{2}$ cup parmesan

salt and pepper

about $\frac{1}{2}$ cup olive oil

2 tablespoons olive oil

300–400g blue cod, or other firm, white-fleshed
  fish, cut into 6 small pieces

seasoned flour for dusting

$\frac{1}{2}$ cup white wine

1 tablespoon butter

lettuce leaves, lemon wedges, green salad and
  fresh crusty bread for serving

THE STORE, KEKERENGU
Seafood Platter

Prepare the gravlax two days before serving. In a shallow dish, lay the salmon fillet skin side down. Sprinkle over the rock salt, pepper, dill, sugar and cognac. Cover the dish tightly with plastic food wrap and leave to marinate in the refrigerator for 2 days before slicing the salmon finely.

To prepare the crayfish, make a court-bouillon in a large stockpot by bringing about 3 cups of water to the boil with the carrots, celery, leek, onion, cayenne pepper, peppercorns, salt and bay leaf. Cook the crayfish, covered, for 5–8 minutes (depending on how well cooked you like the crayfish) in the court-bouillon, remove from the pan and set aside, discarding the liquid.

To prepare the prawns, grill them on a hotplate on the barbecue or in a large frying pan on the stovetop. When just cooked, flambé with the whisky.

To prepare the mussels, steam them open with a small amount of water in a large pot with a lid. Discard any mussels that do not open after 5 minutes. When they are cool enough to handle, break open the shells, leaving the mussel in the half shell. Put a dollop of garlic butter on top of each mussel, then top this with breadcrumbs before grilling under a hot grill until golden. Remove from the oven and set aside.

To prepare the calamari, heat the oil in a frying pan and add the squid rings, garlic and lemon juice and panfry until just cooked. Add parsley and season to taste with salt and pepper, then set aside.

To prepare the fish, firstly make a pesto by placing the basil, walnuts, almonds, garlic and parmesan into the food processor. Season to taste with salt and pepper. Blend together, adding the oil in a steady stream until smooth. Preheat the oven grill. Heat the oil in a frying pan with an ovenproof handle. Coat the blue cod in a little seasoned flour and panfry. When the fish is just cooked, deglaze the pan with the wine and stir in the butter. Spoon the pesto on top of the fish and grill briefly until the pesto is bubbling.

To serve, spread lettuce leaves on the platter and arrange the seafood on top. Serve with lemon wedges, a dressed green salad and fresh crusty bread while the fish is still hot.

MAKES A GENEROUS PLATTER TO SERVE 4–6 PEOPLE

BELOW *The highway and railway run right beside the dramatic and rugged Kaikoura Coast. The wild shore attracts bold surfers to ride the waves. Colonies of fur seals bask on rocks and sea birds wheel overhead.*

WEST COAST

Bounded by the Tasman Sea on one side and the steep mountain slopes of the Southern Alps on the other, the narrow strip that forms the West Coast has a vast reputation for unspoiled wilderness. Lowland dairy farmers enjoy the endless water from the regular rain that makes the grass grow fast and thick.

The West Coast has unique eco systems and each national park has its own distinct terrain, flora and fauna. Kahurangi, in the north, is mountainous with beech forest. Paparoa has extraordinary limestone formations and river plains, whilst the awe-inspiring mountain parks of Arthur's Pass and Mt Aspiring have plant and wildlife habitats up to and beyond the snow line. South Westland is renowned for verdant original rainforest rich in podocarp and ancient trees.

Dispersed along the Coast's main highway are many small towns. Once frontier settlements, these are now adapting to life in the 21st century by offering their own brand of café culture. There are plenty of friendly country pubs, mountain cabins and places to stay off-the-beaten track.

The most notable West Coast delicacy is whitebait, often cooked in pancakes. Dedicated gourmets wait each year for the whitebait season, when these tiny fish are trapped in fine nets at river mouths. Also on the menu are fresh ocean fish caught off the coast and wild venison and pork hunted in the forested hills.

L.R. CAFÉ BAR, KARAMEA
Whitebait Fritters

250g whitebait

2 eggs

1 tablespoon flour

salt and pepper

1 egg white, extra

butter for frying

lemon wedges for serving

fresh green salad and fries for serving

Place the whitebait, whole eggs and flour into a bowl and season to taste with salt and pepper. Beat the extra egg white until fluffy. Melt the butter in a frying pan and while the butter is heating, fold the beaten egg white into the batter. Cook the fritters in batches.

Serve with lemon wedges, a green salad and fries.

SERVES 2

PREVIOUS PAGES West Coast beaches are a roller-coaster of surf and pebbles often misty with salt spray and westerly winds. In places the steep hills dip directly down to the sea.

BELOW Cattle and sheep farming on the West Coast's lowland countryside.

COOKED SALAD DRESSING

25g flour

50g sugar

1 ½ teaspoons mustard powder

¾ teaspoon salt

½ teaspoon white pepper

300ml milk

1 large egg, lightly beaten

2 teaspoons butter

70ml malt vinegar

SALAD

700g new potatoes

3 rashers bacon, rind removed, diced and fried
  until crisp

¾ cup sliced celery

¾ cup diced cucumber

3 tablespoons scissor-snipped chives

2 cloves garlic, crushed

2–3 tablespoons flat-leafed parsley

4 free-range eggs, hardboiled, peeled and sliced

*FAR RIGHT The Buller Gorge road curves
along the forested river canyon linking
Murchison with Westport. Once a scene of
gold fever, the area is now enjoyed for outdoor
pursuits.*

THE SMELTING HOUSE CAFÉ, BARRYTOWN
Eleanor Gray's Potato Salad

To prepare the dressing, place the flour, sugar, mustard powder, salt and white pepper in a heatproof bowl, and mix to a smooth paste with some of the milk. Add the egg and the remainder of the milk. Cook over a pot of simmering water until the dressing is thickened, then add the butter and stir until melted. Lastly stir in the vinegar.

To prepare the salad, cook the potatoes whole with their skins on, and once cool remove the skins and cut into chunks. Place the potatoes along with the bacon, celery, cucumber, chives, garlic and parsley in a bowl and mix together gently. Add the cooked salad dressing and mix in carefully. Lastly add the eggs, taking care not to break them. Refrigerate until ready to serve. Serve in individual salad bowls.

SERVES 4

ABOVE Punakaiki's Pancake Rocks are natural formations of limestone that have been constantly weathered and sculpted by wind and sea. High tides rush under the rocks exploding water spouts up through the blow holes.

The Smelting House Café, Barrytown

Savoury Scones with Sun-dried Tomatoes and Pumpkin Seeds

Preheat the oven to 200°C (190°C fan bake) and grease a baking tray. Sift the flour, baking powder, salt and pepper into the bowl of a food processor, then add the butter. Process until the mixture resembles fine breadcrumbs. Transfer the mixture to a medium-sized bowl. Stir in the cheese, tomato, sun-dried tomatoes, spring onion, basil and pumpkin seeds. Add the milk and mix to a soft dough with a wooden spoon. Knead lightly and flatten to about a 2cm thickness. Cut into shapes using a 5cm biscuit cutter or freehand with a knife. Place on the prepared baking tray leaving a 2cm space between the scones. Brush the tops with milk and sprinkle over a little grated cheese. Bake for 10–15 minutes or until golden brown.

Makes about 12 scones

4 cups plain flour

2 1/2 tablespoons baking powder

3/4 teaspoon salt

1/2 teaspoon freshly ground black pepper

45g butter

3/4 cup grated tasty cheese

1 medium tomato, diced

6 sun-dried tomatoes, diced

1 spring onion, finely sliced

1 teaspoon dried basil

1/4 cup pumpkin seeds

1 1/2 cups milk

extra milk and grated cheese

4 cups peeled, cubed pumpkin

3 tablespoons olive oil

6 cloves garlic, crushed

1/2 teaspoon ground cinnamon

salt and freshly ground black pepper

1 red onion, peeled and chopped

1/2 cup finely shredded basil leaves

1/2 cup pine nuts

1/2 cup pumpkin seeds

4 red peppers (capsicum), roasted and sliced

250g feta cheese

DRESSING

1 1/2 cups olive oil

1 tablespoon balsamic vinegar

1/4 cup white wine vinegar

1 teaspoon wholegrain mustard

salt and freshly ground black pepper

FORMERLY THE BLACKBALL HILTON, BLACKBALL

Feta and Pumpkin Salad

Preheat the oven to 200°C. Place the pumpkin in a roasting dish and drizzle with the olive oil. Sprinkle over the garlic and cinnamon and season to taste with salt and pepper. Roast for about 20 minutes until the pumpkin is cooked through but not too soft. Place the pumpkin in a serving bowl and mix in the red onion, basil, pine nuts, pumpkin seeds, peppers and feta cheese.

To make the dressing, mix all the ingredients together in a blender or shake together in a screw-topped jar. Toss dressing through the salad just before serving.

SERVES 4

NOTE: In the photograph, Feta and Pumpkin Salad is also served with Blackball Bangers (sausages), green salad and potato bake.

LEFT The coal mining town, Blackball,
remains steeped in the past, yet is now known
for its tasty locally-produced Blackball venison
salami. The town is inland from Greymouth
off the Lewis Pass Highway.

RICE SALAD

2 cups white long-grain rice

salt to taste

1 teaspoon turmeric

¼ cup sunflower seeds

¼ cup raisins

SANDFLY STEAKS

1 cup fresh wholemeal breadcrumbs

½ cup fresh fruit, such as apples, pineapple or
   peaches, finely chopped

½ cup chopped fresh basil

squeeze of lemon juice

salt and pepper

1 egg

4 wild pork butterfly schnitzels

2 tablespoons olive oil

1 tablespoon wholegrain mustard

2 cloves garlic, crushed

2 tablespoons plum sauce

½ cup cream

2 tablespoons pine nuts

2 tablespoons pumpkin seeds

2 tablespoons fresh fruit, such as apples,
   pineapple or peaches, chopped

green salad and char-grilled vegetables
   for serving

PUKE PUB LTD, LAKE IANTHE

Sandfly Steaks with Rice Salad

To prepare the rice salad, cook the rice with salt and turmeric using the absorption method. When the rice is almost cooked, add the sunflower seeds and raisins. Set aside.

To prepare the sandfly steaks, mix together the breadcrumbs, fruit, basil and lemon juice and season to taste with salt and pepper. Add the egg to bind the stuffing together. Lay out the pork schnitzels and place a quarter of the stuffing down the centre of each, roll and hold in place with a skewer.

Mix together the oil, mustard and garlic and place in a frying pan over a medium heat. Add the pork to the pan, brush with a little extra olive oil and cook, covered, for about 5 minutes. Remove the lid and cook for a further 5 minutes. Remove the schnitzels and set aside to rest.

Turn up the heat in the pan and deglaze with the plum sauce, then stir in the cream until the sauce thickens.

Arrange each schnitzel on a serving of rice salad, pour over the sauce and sprinkle over pine nuts, pumpkin seeds and chopped fruit. Serve with a tossed green salad and char-grilled vegetables.

SERVES 4

FAR RIGHT Lake Ianthe is 12 kilometres from Ross on Highway 6. Surrounded by ancient forest, the mirror lake has formed in a glacial hole from the ice age.

CANTERBURY

The Canterbury plains stretch between the extraordinary spine of the Southern Alps and the surf-lashed coast of the Pacific Ocean. Neat patchwork fields make up a distinct pattern, often edged by a tall border of shelter trees that emphasise the planned landscape, especially when viewed from above.

On these plains sheep farming is alternated with crops of seeds and grain. Beyond are the foothills of the Alps where run-holders on the high-country stations frequently battle the elements, mustering sheep by horseback and sometimes even by helicopter in order to bring in their huge flocks and cattle herds before winter.

Just an hour's drive out of Christchurch is the village of Akaroa, established by French settlers. The little township exudes Gallic charm through its European cuisine, pretty timber houses with rose gardens and French street names.

Canterbury chefs have a high reputation for award-winning cuisine. Local produce includes salmon from glacier-fed rivers, wild venison, crayfish, grass-fed beef and Canterbury lamb. Close to Christchurch are orchards of apples and pip fruit, boysenberries and raspberries, fresh hazelnuts and walnuts.

PREVIOUS PAGES River terraces of the stony braided Raikaia River spread across the plains, swathing a link with the high country ranges. Merino sheep do well in the higher and cooler alpine pasture, producing the finest of wool, whilst other breeds of sheep are farmed on the lower lands and plains.

ABOVE Ringing in the change of seasons, poplar trees are lime green in spring and brilliant yellow in autumn. Seasonal colours are more dramatic in the South Island, especially in Canterbury and further south.

The Raspberry Café, TAITAPU

Pumpkin, Feta and Pesto Pie

Preheat the oven to 180°C and butter or non-stick spray a deep 23cm flan tin.
To prepare the pastry, place the flour and butter in a food processor and process until they have a breadcrumb consistency. Add the cheese and paprika then with the motor running, dribble in enough cold water until the mixture just comes together. Remove from the food processor and form into a ball on a floured surface. Roll the pastry out so that it overhangs the flan tin. Place the pastry in the refrigerator to chill in the tin. To prepare the filling, toss the pumpkin and red onion in the olive oil, season to taste with sea salt and roast until tender. Mix together the sun-dried tomatoes, eggs, cream, pesto, parsley and chives (if using) and season to taste with sea salt and pepper. Gently stir in the pumpkin and feta. Pour into the prepared pastry shell and arrange overlapping pastry around the sides. Brush visible pastry with egg or milk and bake on a heated tray for about 45–60 minutes or until the filling is set.

SERVES 4–6

PASTRY

2 cups flour

100g butter

1 cup grated tasty cheese

1 teaspoon smoked paprika

about 2 tablespoons cold water

FILLING

about 4 cups 2cm-cubed pumpkin

1 red onion, peeled and roughly chopped

2 tablespoons olive oil

sea salt

handful of sun-dried tomatoes, sliced

6 eggs

1 cup cream

2 tablespoons basil pesto

¼ cup chopped parsley

2 tablespoons chopped chives, optional

sea salt and pepper

1 cup crumbled feta cheese

BASE

150g butter, melted

3 cups plain sweet biscuit, processed
  into crumbs

FILLING

500g cream cheese

250g sour cream

6 eggs

1 cup sugar

1 teaspoon vanilla essence

1 cup white chocolate melts, melted

275g fresh or frozen raspberries

COULIS

275g raspberries

½ cup sugar

cream or yoghurt for serving

THE RASPBERRY CAFÉ, TAITAPU

Baked Raspberry and White Chocolate Cheesecake with Raspberry Coulis

Preheat the oven to 150°C. Butter or non-stick spray a 23cm loose-based cake tin and line the bottom with baking paper.

To prepare the base, mix the butter and biscuit crumbs together and press into the prepared tin. Chill while preparing the filling.

To prepare the filling, place the cream cheese, sour cream, eggs, sugar, vanilla and

RIGHT Canterbury fields are grazed by large flocks of lambs. The high density of sheep to the acre gives New Zealand notoriety for having more sheep than people.

melted chocolate into a food processor and blend until smooth. Pour half the mixture into the chilled base, sprinkle the raspberries over and top with the remaining cream cheese mixture.

To prepare the coulis, place the raspberries and sugar into a food processor and blend until smooth, then sieve to remove the seeds. Drizzle some of the coulis over the cheesecake, reserving some for serving, then bake for 1 hour. Turn off the oven but leave the cheesecake in to cool.

Serve the cheesecake cold with coulis and cream or yoghurt.

SERVES 6–8

4 tortilla shells

2 tablespoons olive oil

1 red pepper (capsicum)

1 green pepper (capsicum)

1 cucumber

2 tomatoes

about 2 cups mesclun lettuce

6 button mushrooms, sliced

4 rashers bacon, sliced

320g smoked chicken, diced

1/2 cup cashew nuts

plain crispy noodles

strawberries to garnish

BALSAMIC DRESSING

100ml balsamic vinegar

1 teaspoon garlic

1 teaspoon wholegrain mustard

3 teaspoons honey

300ml olive oil

salt and pepper

BULLY HAYES, AKAROA
Smoked Chicken Salad

Preheat the oven to 180°C. Brush the tortilla shells with the olive oil and press each shell over a large ovenproof cup. Bake for 8–10 minutes or until golden.

Slice both the peppers in half and remove the core and seeds, then slice into thin strips. Roughly dice the cucumber and cut the tomatoes into wedges. Mix the peppers, cucumber and tomatoes together with the lettuce and set aside.

Place the mushrooms, bacon and chicken into a frying pan and sauté until the bacon is crispy and the chicken heated through.

To prepare the dressing, place the vinegar, garlic, mustard and honey into a bowl and whisk together. Pour the oil into the bowl in a steady stream, whisking continuously until the dressing thickens. Season to taste with salt and pepper and set aside.

To arrange the salad, place 3 tomato wedges on each plate to act as a 'holder' for the tortillas and place a warm tortilla shell in the centre. Fill with the lettuce mixture and sautéed mushrooms, chicken and bacon, then top with cashew nuts and crispy noodles. Garnish with strawberry halves, then drizzle over Balsamic Dressing and serve immediately.

SERVES 4

NOTE: Recipe courtesy of David Sanders.

FAR RIGHT This traditional timber lighthouse was built in the 1880's on the Akaroa Heads. No longer used to guide shipping, it was moved to the beachfront closeby the Akaroa township 100 years later and is now enjoyed for its shape and history.

BELOW The deep, sheltered Akaroa Harbour is fringed by hills. Volcanic loam makes this area very fertile for dairy farming and cheese-making as well as delightful gardens and plant nurseries.

BULLY HAYES, AKAROA

Steamed Green-lipped Mussels

To prepare the tomato sauce, place the onion and garlic in a frying pan and sauté gently until the onion is softened but not brown. Add the curry powder and stir constantly over a moderate heat for about 1 minute. Add the white wine and reduce by two thirds, then add the tomato juice and bring to the boil. Remove from the heat and add the Worcestershire and Tabasco sauces. Set aside.

Steam open the mussels with the white wine in a large frying pan or stockpot with a lid. Discard any mussels that do not open after 5 minutes. Once the mussels are open add the tomato sauce and cover and steam for a further 3 minutes. Remove the mussels from the pan and place into warmed serving bowls. Pour the cream into the pan with the remaining juices and bring to a simmer. Add the fettuccine and heat through. Pour on top of the mussels and garnish with lemon wedges and sliced capsicum. Serve hot with finger bowls.

SERVES 4

NOTE: Recipe courtesy of David Sanders.

TOMATO SAUCE

1 medium onion, peeled and finely chopped

2 teaspoons garlic, crushed

2 teaspoons curry powder

100ml white wine

400ml tomato juice

2 teaspoons Worcestershire sauce

1 teaspoon Tabasco sauce

60 mussels, scrubbed and de-bearded

250ml white wine

100ml cream or coconut cream

400g fettuccine, precooked

lemon wedges and sliced red peppers
 (capsicum) for serving

AVOCADO SALMON ROLL

1 sheet nori, halved

1/3 cup cooked sushi rice (see recipe below)

wasabi paste to taste

2cm-wide slice of salmon fillet, cut across
  the grain

1/2 avocado, thinly sliced

slivers of radish to garnish

RICE PAPER ROLL

1 tablespoon mayonnaise

2 teaspoons soy sauce

1 teaspoon hot chilli sauce

2cm-wide slice of salmon fillet, cut across
  the grain

1 sheet rice paper

iceberg lettuce leaf

4 thin slices cucumber

2 finely sliced onion rings

1 small spring onion, finely sliced lengthways

2 sprigs fresh coriander

1 teaspoon sesame seeds, toasted

NIGIRI SUSHI

15g cooked sushi rice (see recipe below)

wasabi paste to taste

3cm-wide x 12cm-long slice of salmon fillet,
  cut across the grain

SUSHI RICE

2 1/2 cups short grain rice (preferably Koshihikari
  or Sunwhite rice)

1 litre water (1.2–1.3 x the quantity of rice)

100ml vinegar

4 tablespoons sugar

1 tablespoon salt

RIGHT A stone cross makes a dramatic statement against the milky-blue green waters of Lake Tekapo near the tiny Church of the Good Shepherd.

KOHAN RESTAURANT, LAKE TEKAPO
Salmon Sushi Medley

Lay the half sheet of nori shiny side down and spread on the sushi rice to cover the whole surface. Carefully turn the nori and rice over, then spread wasabi down one side of the nori. Lay the salmon piece on top of the wasabi and roll up, starting with the edge nearest you. Layer the avocado slices across the rice roll all the way down the length. Wrap the roll in plastic food wrap and using a bamboo mat (makisu) and three fingers, carefully shape it into a rectangle. Remove the plastic food wrap and cut into 8 pieces using a very sharp knife. Garnish each piece with radish slivers.
MAKES 8 PIECES

Place the mayonnaise, soy sauce and chilli sauce in a flat dish, add the salmon piece and leave to marinate for about a minute. Briefly soak the rice paper in hot water until softened. Layer the lettuce, cucumber, onion, spring onion, coriander and salmon on the rice paper, then sprinkle over the sesame seeds. Roll up tightly and cut into 6 pieces using a very sharp knife.
MAKES 6 PIECES

Shape the rice into a rectangular shape about 6cm long x 2cm wide x 3cm deep, spread with wasabi and press the salmon piece on top in your hands. It will take some practice to master the art of making these nigiri sushi quickly in your hands.
MAKES 1 PIECE

Wash the rice thoroughly, then place into a large bowl, cover with cold water and leave to soak for 30 minutes. Drain off the soaking water, then place into a rice cooker with the litre of water and cook for 30 minutes. Alternatively, cook using the absorption method on the stovetop. Once the rice is cooked, transfer it to a large bowl and add the vinegar, sugar and salt and mix together quickly and thoroughly – be careful not to turn the rice mushy by overmixing. Leave the rice until it is cool enough to handle before using and store in an airtight container with a lid.
MAKES ENOUGH SUSHI RICE FOR 5 PEOPLE

FAR LEFT Milky-turquoise Lake Pukaki rimmed by the outstanding alpine scenery of the Southern Alps. There are more than 14 peaks over 3000 metres and these are topped by Aoraki/Mt Cook at nearly 4000 metres.

THE OLD LIBRARY CAFÉ, FAIRLIE
Potato Pikelets with Mt Cook Smoked Salmon

Preheat the oven to 200°C and grease an oven tray. Place the mashed potatoes, egg yolks, flour and baking powder in a bowl, mix together and season to taste with salt and pepper. In a separate bowl, beat the 3 egg whites stiffly and fold into the potato mixture. Shape the mixture into 8cm x 9cm rounds and place on the prepared oven tray. Bake for 10–12 minutes until golden. Keep warm.

Mix together the sour cream and horseradish.

To serve, place a potato pikelet on each plate, arrange some salad greens and 3 slices of smoked salmon on top, then a dollop of horseradish cream. Top with another pikelet and press down firmly. Garnish with lemon wedges.

The pikelets can be made a day ahead and reheated.

SERVES 4

500g cold cooked potatoes, coarsely mashed

2 eggs, separated

150g plain flour

1/4 teaspoon baking powder

salt and freshly ground pepper

1 egg white, extra

1/2 cup sour cream

horseradish to taste

mixed salad greens for serving

12 slices smoked salmon

lemon to garnish

THE OLD LIBRARY CAFÉ, FAIRLIE

Baked, Peppered Mackenzie Lamb with Potato Rosti and Raspberry Vinaigrette

To prepare the lamb, preheat the oven to 210°C. Mix together the peppercorns, salt and paprika and rub into the lamb rumps. Melt the butter in a frying pan and sear the lamb on all sides, then transfer to a roasting dish and bake for 12–15 minutes, turning halfway through. Cook until the meat is just under medium-rare, then rest it for 7 minutes.

While the lamb is cooking, prepare the raspberry vinaigrette. Place the raspberries (reserving 12 for a garnish) and vinegar in a blender or food processor and blend until smooth. Sieve to remove the seeds, then return to the blender or food processor along with the oil and pepper to taste. Set aside to rest at room temperature. Once the lamb has rested, carve into 8 slices.

To prepare the rosti, peel and coarsely grate the parboiled potatoes and press into egg rings. Melt the butter in a frying pan and cook each rosti until golden. Season to taste with salt and pepper and set aside to rest.

To serve, arrange a potato rosti on each plate with several slices of lamb on top. Pile the salad greens on the side of the plate. Drizzle the raspberry vinaigrette over the salad, beside the potato and lamb, and garnish with the reserved raspberries.

SERVES 4

LAMB

50g finely ground black peppercorns

1 teaspoon salt

1/2 teaspoon ground paprika

4 whole lamb rumps, trimmed of any excess fat and sinew

1–2 tablespoons butter

RASPBERRY VINAIGRETTE

200g raspberries, fresh or frozen

200ml raspberry vinegar, or cider vinegar plus 1/2 teaspoon sugar

100ml olive oil

freshly ground black pepper

POTATO ROSTI

2 large potatoes, unpeeled and parboiled

50g butter

salt and pepper

salad greens for serving

FAR LEFT Aoraki/Mt Cook at 3746 metres is the tallest mountain in Australasia. Nearby, the small Mt Cook village has a visitor centre with information on the National Park's flora, fauna and geology.

BATTER

75g sugar

3 eggs

260g flour

1/2 teaspoon baking powder

250g milk

50g butter, melted and cooled slightly

BERRY COULIS

1/2 punnet strawberries, hulled

30g sugar

water

1 punnet strawberries, extra, hulled and
  quartered

butter for frying

4 scoops ice cream

150ml crème pâtissière or custard, thick enough
  so it won't run onto the plate

icing sugar for dusting

THE OLD LIBRARY CAFÉ, FAIRLIE
Strawberry Pancakes

To prepare the batter, cream the sugar and the eggs together in a bowl. Whisk in the flour, baking powder and milk, then stir in the cooled melted butter. Set aside to rest while you prepare the coulis.

To prepare the coulis, blend the half punnet of strawberries with the sugar and enough water to make a thick coulis. Sieve to remove the seeds and gently stir through the strawberry quarters. Set aside.

Heat the butter in a frying pan and pour in the batter to make 4 large pancakes, frying each side until golden. Roll each pancake into a cornet shape and hold it in place with a toothpick. Place a scoop of ice cream inside each pancake, then a spoonful of crème pâtissière or custard, then a spoonful of strawberry coulis. Lastly, pour over the remaining crème pâtissière or custard and dust with icing sugar. If you prefer, you can replace the toothpicks with toffee spikes.

SERVES 4

BELOW Hot dry summers turn the pastoral farmland to golden brown in sheep country near Geraldine and Fairlie. These rural townships serve the high country sheep stations on the foothills of the Southern Alps.

OTAGO &
SOUTHLAND

Wide open spaces and huge horizons typify the breathtaking landscapes of Otago and Southland. Southern cities and towns with their imposing stately homes and heritage buildings were once among the most prosperous in New Zealand. These days small country towns have a hard-won reputation for country music, home brew and sometimes even moonshine. Bluff is a fishing settlement whilst Alexandra, Cardrona and Cromwell, once flush with gold fever, are now better known for their vineyards, orchards and blossom festivals.

The region's mouth-watering seafood is harvested from deep in the Southern Ocean. Bluff oysters have a reputation as the sweetest and most succulent in the country and southern fishermen brave the elements for crayfish and paua, tuna, orange roughy and blue cod. All of these local delicacies are readily available to taste and enjoy.

DRESSING

3 tablespoons ABC sweet soy sauce

1 tablespoon fish sauce

1 tablespoon sweet chilli sauce

1 tablespoon light soy sauce

2cm piece lemongrass

2cm piece ginger

4 cloves garlic

2 tablespoons sesame oil

SALAD

1/2 red pepper (capsicum), thinly sliced

1/2 yellow pepper (capsicum), thinly sliced

1/2 green pepper (capsicum), thinly sliced

1 red onion, peeled and thinly sliced

1 spring onion, thinly sliced

1 leek, thinly sliced and lightly sautéed

1 carrot, thinly sliced

1/2 cucumber, thinly sliced

1/4 cup roughly chopped Vietnamese mint

1/4 cup roughly chopped fresh coriander

1/4 cup roughly chopped fresh basil

200g rare beef, thinly sliced

1 packet vermicelli noodles, deep-fried

fried shallots, fresh coriander and a squeeze
  of fresh lime juice for serving

PREVIOUS PAGES Extensive sheep runs in the high country have their own way of life. Many farm merino sheep for the fine and exclusive wool now used by some of the world's most influential fashion houses in Europe.

FAR RIGHT Moody stillness across Lake Wanaka, one of the larger lakes of the southern region. In summer the lake is a playground for fishing and boating. In winter the nearby mountains are snow covered and popular for skiing and snow-boarding.

RITUAL ESPRESSO CAFÉ, WANAKA
Thai Beef Salad

Prepare the dressing by processing all the ingredients in a food processor or blender. Add a little water if it is too strong.

Place all the vegetables, herbs, beef and dressing in a large salad bowl and toss together to combine.

To serve, place the noodles on a plate and top with the beef and vegetables. Garnish with fried shallots, coriander and lime juice.

SERVES 2

CARDRONA HOTEL, CARDRONA
Ostrich Fillet on a Peppered Potato Rosti with a Port and Rosemary Glaze

2 large potatoes

salt to taste

cracked black pepper

1 tablespoon finely chopped fresh rosemary

oil for frying

800g ostrich eye-fillet

2 tablespooons port

2 teaspoons chopped fresh rosemary, extra

300ml reduced beef stock

1 tablespoon butter

freshly steamed vegetables for serving

Preheat the oven to 180°C. To prepare the rosti, grate the potatoes into a clean cloth or tea towel, sprinkle over salt and wring out as much liquid as possible. Mix cracked pepper to taste and the first measure of rosemary through the potato. Heat the oil in a frying pan until it is smoking, then add all the potato mixture and fry until golden brown. Flip once and brown the other side. Transfer to an ovenproof dish and place in the oven for about 10–15 minutes or until cooked through. Set aside.

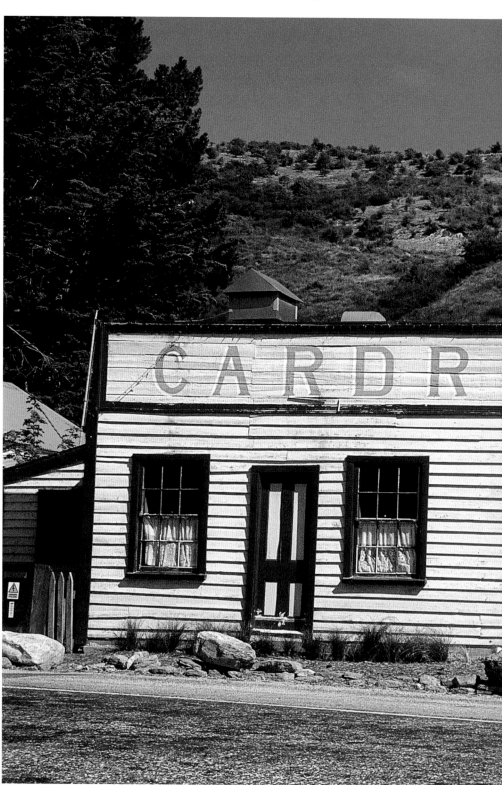

RIGHT The historic Cardrona Hotel where skiers and tourists dine and imbibe. Once on the site of an old gold town, this hotel is the last remnant from an earlier era.

Slice the ostrich fillet into medallions and panfry for a few minutes on each side, depending on how you like your meat. Medium-rare to rare is the best as the meat is very lean. Once the meat is cooked remove from the pan and set aside to rest.

Turn up the heat and deglaze the pan with the port and remaining rosemary, then add the stock and simmer until the liquid has reduced by about a third. Stir through the butter.

To serve, arrange freshly steamed vegetables on each plate and place several medallions on top. Cut the rosti into 4 portions and place beside the meat, then pour over the sauce.

SERVES 4

CARDRONA HOTEL, CARDRONA

Lemon Pannacotta

Lightly oil four ramekins or moulds. Place the cream, sugar, lemon zest, vanilla bean and lemon into a saucepan and gently bring to the boil. Soak the gelatine in a little water to soften, then add the gelatine to the hot cream and stir to dissolve. Strain the liquid to remove the vanilla bean and lemon and add the Limoncello. Pour the warm mixture into the prepared dishes and leave to set in the refrigerator for at least 8 hours, preferably overnight.

Serve chilled with fresh berries or a fruit compote and garnish with caramelised sugar and mint or flowers if using.

SERVES 4

300ml cream

3 tablespoons caster sugar

1/2 teaspoon finely grated lemon zest

1/2 vanilla bean

1/2 lemon

1 1/2 gelatine leaves

1/2 tablespoon Limoncello

fresh berries or fruit compote for serving

caramelised sugar and mint or flowers
  to garnish (optional)

BELOW The notoriously steep Crown Range road with several hairpin bends links Queenstown with Wanaka and provides access to the Cardrona and Waiorau skifields.

FLEUR'S PLACE, MOERAKI
Chunky Seafood Chowder

150g butter

4 carrots, roughly chopped

2 onions, peeled and roughly chopped

3 sticks celery, roughly chopped

4 medium-sized potatoes, peeled and roughly
  chopped

2 cups tomato paste

2–3 cups flour

10 litres fish stock (see note)

1kg mixture of bite-sized chunks of local fish
  and seafood: lemon fish, John dory, cod,
  warehou, mussels, squid, baby octopus, etc

salt and pepper

fresh chives, uncut, to garnish

crusty fresh bread for serving

Melt the butter in a large saucepan and add the vegetables and tomato paste. Cook for about 6–8 minutes to soften the vegetables, then slowly add the flour to make a roux. Turn down the heat and slowly add the stock, allowing it to thicken as you go and stirring continuously to avoid lumps. Add the fish and seafood and bring to the boil, then simmer until everything is cooked. Season to taste with salt and pepper, garnish with chives and serve hot with crusty fresh bread.

SERVES 6–8

NOTE: Fleur's Place fish stock is made from the heads and bodies of fresh local blue cod that is simmered for several hours with black peppercorns, salt and bay leaves. Alternatively you could use a good-quality commercial fish stock.

ABOVE The extraordinary, round Moeraki boulders are naturally formed from ancient sea sediments. Erosion action by the waves has gradually exposed them on the beach and foreshore.

FLEUR'S PLACE, MOERAKI
Whole Lemon Sole, Fresh from the *Charlotte Rose*

Preheat the oven to 200°C. Clarify the butter by melting in a small saucepan and boiling gently until the top white fat has disappeared, leaving a clear, light golden liquid. Place the fish on a baking tray basted with clarified butter and bake for 10–15 minutes or until cooked.
Serve with fresh local vegetables panfried in clarified butter.
SERVES 1

2 tablespoons butter

1 whole lemon sole or flounder

fresh vegetables for serving

BELOW The fishing village of Moeraki on a tiny sheltered harbour 80 kilometres north of Dunedin. Fishing craft set out into the nearby Pacific Ocean to catch sole, blue cod and orange roughy.

CAREYS BAY HISTORIC HOTEL, CAREYS BAY

Spinach and Ricotta Cannelloni

SAUCE

575g can tomatoes

1 medium onion, peeled

olive oil for frying

salt

FILLING

300g spinach

400g ricotta cheese

50g freshly grated parmesan cheese

1 egg

1 egg yolk

salt

¹/₂ teaspoon freshly grated nutmeg

12 cannelloni tubes, precooked

extra freshly grated parmesan cheese
  for sprinkling

fresh salad and roasted potatoes for serving

To prepare the sauce, crush the tomatoes or blend them briefly, finely chop the onion and coat the base of a large frying pan with olive oil. When the pan is hot but not smoking, add the onion and fry gently until it is transparent. Add the tomatoes and simmer for about 20 minutes, adding salt to taste and stirring occasionally to prevent sticking. Preheat the oven to 200°C. To prepare the filling, cook the spinach briefly in boiling, salted water and drain well, squeezing out most of the water. Finely chop the spinach. Pass the ricotta through a sieve and add the chopped spinach, parmesan, egg, egg yolk, salt to taste and grated nutmeg. Mix together thoroughly. Fill the cannelloni tubes with the spinach and ricotta filling and arrange them in an ovenproof dish. Pour over the tomato sauce and sprinkle with extra parmesan. Bake at the top of the oven for about 20 minutes or until the cannelloni have heated through and the cheese is golden. Serve hot with a fresh salad and roasted potatoes.

SERVES 4

BELOW The Otago Harbour, with Dunedin at its head, is sheltered by a rim of volcanic hills. Cruise vessels ply the harbour offering views of the harbour and wildlife nearby.

NIAGARA FALLS CAFÉ, TOKANUI

Shearer's Stew

Heat the first measure of butter in a large pot and gently fry the onions and garlic until transparent. Toss the steak pieces in flour and melt the 50g butter in a frying pan. Fry the meat in batches on a moderate–high heat until lightly browned. Add the meat to the pot with the onions and garlic. Stir in the wine, stock, tomato paste and mixed herbs and gently bring to the boil, stirring continuously, then add the carrots, swede, potatoes, beans and season to taste with salt and pepper. Reduce the heat to low and simmer for about 2 hours or until the meat is tender, stirring occasionally.
Serve in bowls with garlic bread or huge chunks of fresh bread smothered in butter.

SERVES 6 BLOKES

2–3 tablespoons butter

2 medium onions, peeled and chopped

4 cloves garlic, crushed

1.5kg stewing steak, cut into man-sized bites

flour for dusting

50g butter

1 1/2 cups red wine

1 1/2 cups beef stock

1/4 cup tomato paste

1 teaspoon dried mixed herbs

6 carrots, peeled and sliced

3 cups peeled, diced swede

2 cups peeled, diced potatoes

2 cups beans, sliced

salt and pepper

garlic or fresh bread for serving

OPTIONAL EXTRAS

bacon

cabbage

mushrooms

pumpkin

shearer's singlet

fleece with dags removed

one huntaway dog

NIAGARA FALLS CAFÉ, TOKANUI
Bumblebees

Preheat the oven to 160°C and butter or non-stick spray a baking tray. Mix all the ingredients together, then roll into golf ball-sized balls with your hands. Place on the prepared tray. If you find the mixture sticking to your hands rinse your hands under the tap first and shake off excess moisture. Bake for 15 minutes or until lightly golden. Loosen the Bumblebees as soon as you remove them from the oven to prevent sticking. Cool on a wire cake rack.

MAKES ABOUT 14

3 cups dried fruit, any combination including nuts — I use the following: 1 ½ cups chopped dates, ½ cup raisins, ½ cup currants, ½ cup mixed peel

1 can sweetened condensed milk

3 cups coconut

LEFT Southland's wide open spaces are farmed in huge sheep and cattle stations. In the summer, high country pasture is used then, before winter, sheep are mustered and brought down to the lowlands.

CATLINS FARMSTAY, PROGRESS VALLEY, CATLINS

Corned Silverside with Mustard Sauce, Roasted Beets and Carrots

corned silverside, about 800g

1 tablespoon golden syrup

ROASTED BEETROOT AND CARROTS

4–5 medium beetroot

5 large carrots

2 tablespoons olive oil

1 tablespoon brown sugar

1 tablespoon balsamic vinegar

1/2 cup fresh orange juice

salt and pepper

MUSTARD SAUCE

1 1/2 cups liquid the corned beef was cooked in

2 dessertspoons cornflour

2 tablespoons vinegar

1 teaspoon mustard

1 egg

1 dessertspoon sugar

fresh vegetables for serving

To prepare the corned beef, place the corned silverside in a large pot and just cover with cold water. Add the golden syrup and bring to the boil, then reduce the heat and simmer gently until tender, about an hour. Leave to rest in the cooking liquid. Preheat the oven to 180°C. To prepare the beetroot and carrots, peel and cut them into

RIGHT Sheepdogs working in the Catlins area south of Dunedin. Throughout New Zealand farmers use whistle calls to instruct sheepdogs to move flocks of sheep, both in the yards and around huge paddocks.

batons the size of your little finger. Place in a roasting dish with the olive oil, brown sugar, vinegar and orange juice, mix well and spread out in the dish. Season to taste with salt and pepper. Roast for about an hour until tender. Serve hot or cold.

To prepare the mustard sauce, place all the ingredients together in a saucepan and cook for a few minutes, stirring continuously until thickened.

Serve the sliced corned beef hot or cold with mustard sauce, roasted beetroot and carrots and fresh vegetables on the side.

SERVES 4

RESTAURANT GUIDE

Since *Country New Zealand* was first printed, some of the restaurants have closed, but we have kept the recipes in because they are so good! A number of other restaurants have changed names, and their new details are included below.

FAR NORTH

BOATSHED CAFÉ AND CRAFTS, 8 Clendon Esplanade, Rawene, ph 09 405 7728
SLUNG ANCHOR RESTAURANT AND BAR, 10 Waterfront Drive, Mangonui, ph 09 406 1233
TUNA CAFÉ, 67–69 Main Road, Moerewa, ph 09 404 0304

AUCKLAND & COROMANDEL

BEESONLINE HONEY CENTRE AND CAFÉ, 791 State Highway 16, Waimauku, ph 09 411 7953
THE CHURCH RESTAURANT, 87 Beach Road, Hahei, ph 07 866 3797
CLEVEDON CAFÉ, 1 North Road, Clevedon, ph 09 292 8111
GRANGE ROAD CAFÉ, 7 Grange Road, Hahei, ph 07 866 3502
HERON'S FLIGHT WINERY AND CAFÉ, 49 Sharp Road, Matakana, ph 09 422 7915
SOLA CAFÉ, 720B Pollen St, Thames, ph 07 868 8781

WAIKATO & CENTRAL NORTH ISLAND

PEARL'S CAFÉ AND RESTAURANT (*formerly* BANCO), 174 Whitaker Street, Te Aroha, ph 07 884 7574
MAORIFOOD.COM, PO Box 1030, Rotorua, ph 07 345 3122
REPLETE FOOD COMPANY, 45 Heu Heu Street, Taupo, ph 07 378 0606
RIVER VALLEY VENTURES LTD, Pukeokahu R D 2, Taihape, ph 06 388 1444
TONGUE AND GROOVE CAFÉ, 19 Bow Street, Raglan, ph 07 825 0027
WORKMANS CAFÉ BAR, 52 Broadway, Matamata, ph 07 888 5498

EASTERN NORTH ISLAND

HEP-SET MOOCH CAFÉ, 58 West Quay, Napier, ph 06 834 2336
HIGHGATE, 2115 Wharerata Road, Gisborne, ph 06 862 8435
WHITEBAY WORLD OF LAVENDER, 527 Main Road, Eskdale, Napier, ph 06 836 6553

TARANAKI

CAFÉ WUNDERBAR, 1129 Main South Road, Oakura, ph 06 752 7303
KAURI COTTAGE CAFÉ RESTAURANT, 1281 Egmont Road, Egmont Village, ph 06 752 2757
TAWA GLEN CAFÉ AND GARDEN CENTRE, 450 Mountain Road, Lepperton, ph 06 752 0809
WAIAU ESTATE CAFÉ AND WINERY, 9 Onaero Beach Road, Onaero, ph 06 752 3609

MANAWATU & WAIRARAPA

EKETAHUNA COUNTRY CAFÉ AND CRAFTS, 24 Main Street, Eketahuna, ph 06 375 8272

THE OLD WINERY CAFÉ, Cnr Ponatahi and Huangarua Roads, Martinborough, ph 06 306 8333

SUNDANCE CAFÉ, 16 Ocean Beach Road, Foxton Beach, ph 06 363 5091

TOAD'S LANDING, Pokohiwi Road, Masterton, ph 06 377 3793

'THE WOOLSHEDS', Amalgamated Helicopters Ltd, 145 Chester Road, Carterton, Masterton, ph 06 379 8600

NELSON, MARLBOROUGH & KAIKOURA

LE CAFÉ, 12–14 London Quay, Picton, ph 03 573 5588

MORRISON STREET CAFÉ, 244 Hardy Street, Nelson, ph 03 548 8110

SHED 1 (*formerly* FLAX), Mapua Wharf, Mapua, Nelson, ph 03 540 2028

HOOKED ON MARAHAU, Sandy Bay Road, Marahau, ph 03 527 8576

THE STORE, State Highway 1, Kekerengu, ph 03 575 8600

WEST COAST

FORMERLY THE BLACKBALL HILTON, 26 Hart Street, Blackball, ph 03 732 4705

L. R. CAFÉ BAR, 71 Waverly Street, Karamea, ph 03 782 6616

PUKE PUB LTD, Pukekura, Lake Ianthe, ph 03 755 4144

THE SMELTING HOUSE CAFÉ, 102 MacKay Street, Barrytown, ph 03 768 0012

CANTERBURY

BULLY HAYES, 57 Beach Road, Akaroa, ph 03 304 7533

KOHAN RESTAURANT, Main Street (State Highway 8), Lake Tekapo, ph 03 680 6688

THE OLD LIBRARY CAFÉ, 6 Allandale Road, Fairlie, ph 03 685 8999

THE RASPBERRY CAFÉ, Rhodes Road, Taitapu, ph 03 329 6979

OTAGO & SOUTHLAND

CARDRONA HOTEL, Crown Range Road, Cardrona, ph 03 443 8153

CAREYS BAY HISTORIC HOTEL, 17 MacAndrew Road, Careys Bay, Dunedin, ph 03 472 8022

CATLINS FARMSTAY, 174 Progress Valley Road, Catlins, ph 03 246 8843

FLEUR'S PLACE, 169 Haven Street, Moeraki, ph 03 439 4480

NIAGARA FALLS CAFÉ, 256 Niagara Waikawa Road, Tokanui, ph 03 246 8577

RITUAL ESPRESSO CAFÉ, 18 Helwick Street, Wanaka, ph 03 443 6662

INDEX